The slow death of great cities?

Urban abandonment or urban renaissance

Anne Power and Katharine Mumford

The Joseph Rowntree Foundation has supported this project as part of its programme of research and innovative development projects, which it hopes will be of value to policy makers and practitioners. The facts presented and views expressed in this report are, however, those of the authors and not necessarily those of the Foundation.

Photographs are © Anthony Lee (LSE Housing) and Katharine Mumford

The flyer on page 34 is reproduced courtesy of City of Newcastle upon Tyne Housing Department; the photographs on page 79 are reproduced courtesy of Urban Splash; Appendix 6 is reproduced courtesy of Manchester City Council.

Published for the Joseph Rowntree Foundation by YPS

ISBN 1 902633 11 3

Cover design by Adkins Design

Prepared and printed by:
York Publishing Services Ltd
64 Hallfield Road
Layerthorpe
York YO31 7ZQ

Contents

Acknowledgements

The debt of thanks we owe to staff and residents in the cities of Manchester and Newcastle, particularly in the four case study areas, is immeasurable. We cannot name most of our local collaborators in order to protect the identity of the areas. We have tried to do justice to their trust and confidence. Without them, we would not have understood how serious the problem of urban abandonment was, nor how intense the commitment to help. We would also like to thank Kevin Lavery (Chief Executive), David Butler (Director of Housing), John Cornhill (Assistant Director), Paul Tanney (Principal Housing Manager), Michael Kerridge (Housing Needs Manager) in Newcastle City Council; and Howard Bernstein (Chief Executive), Steve Mycio (Deputy Chief Executive (Performance)), Fionnuala Stringer (Principal Team Leader), Clare Tostevin (Low Demand Team Leader) in Manchester City Council. We are also grateful to staff in all the other councils and housing associations who co-operated with our study. We are greatly indebted to Anthony Lee who helped with the fieldwork interviews and Rebecca Morris who prepared the report for publication.

We must also thank Mavis McDonald (DETR), Anthony Mayer and Max Steinberg (Housing Corporation), Moira Wallace and Liz Walton (Social Exclusion Unit) for their support in organising three workshops on low demand and unpopular areas. These involved over 100 participants from all over the country, giving us many additional sources of information and ideas of what can be done to change conditions.

Finally, we thank Theresa McDonagh, John Lowe, Richard Best, Alan Holmans, Rebecca Tunstall, Ruth Lupton, Ade Kearns, Alan Kilburn, Jackie Haq, Chris Power, Mike Gahagan, Ivan Turok and Duncan Maclennan who gave excellent advice and painstakingly helped us to draft, correct and recorrect the text of this report. We also want to thank John Stevens and Barbara Carlisle for their support on the advisory committee.

We accept full and sole responsibility for any mistakes or misrepresentations in discussing what has proved to be a highly topical and therefore contentious issue.

Definitions

Abandonment describes a house which is empty and which no one wants to use or live in; also whole areas of empty housing – 'area abandonment'. 'Abandonment' can be caused by the occupier vacating a property without giving any notice, or by the owner, believing the property to have zero or negative value.

Brownfield describes land that has already been used for development. It is usually in towns and cities but airfields, army camps and other previously developed land in villages and the country, and along roads, railways and canals are included. Local authorities have a target of producing 60 per cent of new housing on brownfield sites. Renovation of existing buildings and change of use (e.g. offices to flats) come within the brownfield category.

Census information in the report is based on official Census definitions.

Changing demand implies different groups seeking access, e.g. singles or families, young or elderly, ethnic minorities or whites. It may result in housing being used in a different way, e.g. temporary rather than permanent housing.

City council and government information is based on the definitions in their documents. These are fully referenced.

Difficult to let describes rented housing which has above average refusal rates, turnover and empty property but below average demand or waiting lists. The term was first used in 1976 when the then Labour government mounted the investigation of difficult to let housing (Burbidge *et al.*, 1981).

General Improvement Areas (GIAs) were introduced by the 1969 Housing Act. Run-down inner city areas were designated for conservation through improvement grants to individual owners and environmental grants to

local authorities to upgrade the area as a whole. They ranged from 300–800 homes. Some were sold off at great profits to owner occupiers.

Gentrification describes the improvement of decayed inner city housing through more affluent owners buying run-down, older property and doing it up. The term suggests lower income people losing out in the process.

Greenfield describes land that has not been built on (generally within living memory) or that bears no sign of construction. Greenfield housing developments are exempt from VAT.

Housing Action Areas (HAAs) were set up through the 1974 Housing Act. They were a response to 'gentrification' and combined council action with bottom-up methods to tackle inner city decline in small areas of around 500 properties. Declared areas attracted generous improvement grants aimed at encouraging residents to stay. Tenants' rights were guaranteed and, where private landlords failed to improve, councils could compulsorily purchase and renovate.

Inner Urban Areas define the distinct parts of the city around the city centre characterised by above average concentrations of social and economic problems. The exact definition varies but the same areas with similar characteristics, in the same cities, tend to reappear on all indices and definitions (see DoE, 1996, p. 211).

Low demand describes housing which few people want to move into, or remain living in. The term applies to owner occupied as well as rented housing. It underlines the possibility of choice in where people live. It applies to areas where overall demand is low relative to supply, suggesting an emerging surplus of housing. The areas affected can be small neighbourhoods, estates, cities or whole districts. The term is sometimes applied to regions such as the North East or Merseyside.

Negative equity means that a property has a lower market value than the outstanding debt the owner has incurred in buying the property.

New Deal for Communities (NDC) was launched in September 1998 as the most recent regeneration programme. It proposes neighbourhood management of up to 4,500 homes, co-ordinating health, education, police, training, security, family support and housing. It offers significant capital resources, but also funds resident consultation, capacity building and long-term support. NDC encourages innovative models of ownership, management and involvement.

Outer Urban Areas are those areas within city boundaries, further from the centre, with less concentrated problems and more attractive environments (see DoE, 1996, p. 211).

Single Regeneration Budget (SRB) brought together 20 programmes run through various government departments. It creates local partnerships – private/public/statutory/ voluntary – to deliver large- and small-scale regeneration covering environment, security, training, employment, commerce, leisure and, in a minority of cases, housing.

Social exclusion describes the processes which reduce or limit people's life chances, resulting in some individuals and groups being unable to participate fully in the society in which they live.

Social Exclusion Unit was set up by the new Labour government in 1997 to co-ordinate different government efforts in tackling the problems that place some people outside mainstream society. The first three priorities were truancy and school exclusion, street living and the most disadvantaged neighbourhoods. Cross-departmental action teams including non-governmental experts are expected to propose new 'joined-up' solutions.

Turnover means the rate of exodus from an area based on the numbers of households leaving as a percentage of all occupied units.

Urban Development Corporations (UDCs) were established by the 1980 Local Government and Land Act. They took over planning powers from the local authority for designated inner city areas with an obsolete industrial, manufacturing infrastructure. Their aim was to lever in private investment through strong public support to create new and refurbished commercial and residential centres.

Zero demand is housing which no one wants, for which there is no waiting list or market value.

Executive summary

Problems

This report examines the experience of four neighbourhoods within the inner areas of two Northern cities that suffer from low demand, incipient abandonment and general depopulation. Their problems reflect much wider trends. Many city neighbourhoods experience acute decline and, in the most extreme cases, abandonment. Layers of regeneration programmes have made some improvements but underlying problems continue unchanged.

Manchester and Newcastle have declined over much of this century. Their populations have dropped as jobs have disappeared. Deprivation is heavily concentrated within the cities, but particularly within the inner neighbourhoods. Large clusters of poverty and unemployment have formed across wide areas involving hundreds of thousands of households. Concentrated deprivation is regarded as the single biggest factor in area decline in both cities.

The quality of most housing in the areas is good, much of it excellent. But abandonment is affecting all tenures and all property types. Council housing forms the largest tenure in the neighbourhoods but there is significant owner occupation and some private renting. Housing associations have been very active in the 1980s and 1990s. Renting dominates and helps determine who lives in the areas. Younger people in work tend to move out to buy.

The four neighbourhoods traditionally housed low-income people. The chronic job losses and the cumulative impact of urban depopulation have led to empty unwanted property becoming a blight on the areas over the last five years. The value of private property has plummeted in the 1990s, in some cases to zero. Right to Buy sales are far below the average for the cities, which in turn are far below national levels. Turnover is exceptionally high, making effective management and community stability elusive goals.

Demolition has removed several thousand properties in the two cities, particularly in the inner neighbourhoods, but numbers of empty properties have not declined. In some areas they have continued to grow. Whole streets are sometimes abandoned and the areas are dotted with empty unused spaces. Demolition decisions are often a piecemeal reaction to intense problems rather than part of a renewal plan. The blight and uncertainty of demolition fuel the exodus of those that can.

Schools have been seriously affected. Pupil turnover and falling roles have had a negative effect even where schools are performing well. This in turn undermines neighbourhood cohesion. Crime and disturbance are major problems but intensive, proactive policing and collaboration with residents and local housing managers have cut crime and created more peaceful conditions in some areas.

The main factors associated with acute decline are: poor reputation and negative history; surplus rented housing coupled with declining populations; neighbourhood management problems; disrupted communities with weak social controls; acute harassment and anti-social behaviour; a clustering of pressures provoking a cumulative crisis.

Low demand is most extensive in council estates, and there is evidence of falling and changing demand for social housing in many areas of the country – in regions of housing shortage as well as surplus. Local authorities and housing associations in different regions report increasing turnover and numbers of difficult to let properties, and changing social and demographic profiles of applicants.

Prospects

The study uncovered hundreds of projects and programmes underway within the neighbourhoods, most of them small scale, in an attempt to hold on to conditions. Without these initiatives, social problems would be much worse. In some cases they are having a measurable effect. For example, strong enforcement has cut crime; private developers have sold new homes to incomers; residents and housing staff within small areas have organised local compacts that have increased security, involvement, service quality and stability.

There are many positive new ideas currently on trial: a strong pro-urban stance; an array of innovative, experimental government initiatives targeted at the most deprived areas; a focus on community and environmental conditions; a strong emphasis on bottom-up approaches, creating many local avenues for inventiveness and using many local levers to prevent a slide into abandonment; a commitment from the local authorities to rebuild inner neighbourhoods after the devastation left by the collapse in manufacturing; a re-emphasis on core services, such as schools, police, health; a neighbourhood management focus; and a determined approach to centre city revitalisation that could spread to the inner neighbourhoods.

The biggest challenges for cities are: attracting back more people in work on higher incomes and with higher skills; developing the skills and confidence of existing residents and linking them into new work opportunities; stabilising community conditions and preventing further exodus; creating strong neighbourhood management structures that can co-ordinate and deliver programmes, enforce basic conditions and maintain core services; addressing the inner city environment – street cleaning, refuse, repair, lack of greenery, traffic.

New experimental forms of city regeneration are popular and are attracting more and more new residents into city centres. The seeming contradiction between urban abandonment and urban renaissance represents two sides of a single coin. Inner areas are adjacent to successful new developments in core city areas. Inner city neighbourhoods have many assets including space, infrastructure, proximity, and quality housing. Strong universal underpinning such as education, targeted programmes to equalise the poorest areas, and a commitment to existing residents could unleash the potential for inner area regrowth.

1 Introduction – urban abandonment or urban renaissance?

Why do some cities and their neighbourhoods generate abandonment, chaos, breakdown at the same time as they display resilience, experiment, innovation, excitement? Cities have the brightest lights and the darkest corners, feeding the hopes and fuelling the fears of millions. In this report, we examine a national problem of urban decay in the light of the experience of two great cities suffering acute decline and four neighbourhoods witnessing the growing abandonment of sound property. Managers in the cities we study talk about the abandoned terraces and rejected streets of inner neighbourhoods in terms of death and disease – 'they're finished', 'there's nothing more we can do', 'we can't save it', 'it's a cancer', 'it has to go', 'it's damaging nearby areas', 'the voids have bred'.

Britain ran the largest slum clearance programme in the western world after the Second World War. Yet, we are contemplating new urban clearances. We are demolishing thousands of the very homes we built to replace those slums.

In every major British city every year – London, Birmingham, Liverpool, Manchester, Newcastle, Glasgow, and many smaller cities besides – we are wiping out housing we say we need. Why? Too few people want to live in urban areas in many parts of the country. The neighbourhoods that are depopulating most rapidly create a feeling of lifelessness in spite of the efforts of residents and landlords as well as most other agencies in the city. The abandoned buildings look like graves; the new railings, lighting, planting, play areas like flowers on gravestones, a lingering farewell to something loved now lost. The signs of care survive but many of the people have gone.

Lavishing care on slowing the death of the most difficult urban neighbourhoods is a statement about the future, just as flowers are an affirmation of hope. It is obvious to an observer that these areas should not just waste away. Our study reinforces the urgency of the urban agenda because of the risk that abandonment and subsequent demolition may spread much further. Unlike human deaths, no one is recording the numbers, the cause, or the impact on cities as a whole, of neighbourhood abandonment and renewed demolition. Demolition may be like some ritual bleeding – the more we knock down, the more people continue to seep away.

This report attempts to do three things – uncover and explain those events that are combining to cause the abandonment of urban neighbourhoods; describe the struggle of those living through the experience; uncover and assess attempted remedies and their impact on conditions and trends.

Neither slums nor city decay are inevitable. They are man-made problems. But, if we knew how to keep poor city neighbourhoods working, our search for the reason why and the way out would be simple. It is far from simple. We met a barrage of opinions, emotions and evidence of conflicting trends. The 'inevitability of abandonment', the 'uncontrollability of decline' at ground level were matched by optimistic predictions of population growth, job expansion and rebirth at the most senior city hall level.

Most abandoned housing is structurally sound and, in more popular neighbourhoods, it would unquestionably stay up and be worth a lot of money. Is demolition inevitable? Is pruning back cities the right approach to allow space for renewed growth? Or does gentrification work? The process transforms old and valueless neighbourhoods into sought-after areas of rising value through the injection of investment and the attraction of better off people. This process rescued the depopulating slum clearance areas of Islington and turned them into some of the most highly prized London neighbourhoods (Ferris, 1972). Can we learn anything from the semi-abandoned Georgian and Victorian slums we saved from the bulldozer 30 years ago?

We found evidence of low demand in the South East and South West as well as the Midlands and North. Housing associations are beginning to encounter letting difficulties, until recently found only in local authorities. Owner occupiers in poor neighbourhoods face long-run negative equity and devaluation of their property.

Can an urban renaissance work for deprived neighbourhoods so that the space and opportunity within cities created by long-run decline generate momentum for rebirth? The findings from our research reinforce the potential for city regrowth.

The report is divided into five parts.

- Part I explains the background and approach to the study, describing the main demographic, economic, social and housing patterns of the cities of Newcastle, Manchester and four unpopular neighbourhoods within them.

- Part II presents evidence of acute decline and incipient abandonment in the cities and neighbourhoods we studied in detail, and in other parts of the country where we sought evidence of the problem.

- Part III tells the story of four communities, relying on the direct evidence we collected during visits and talking to around 120 local people living and working with the problems.

- Part IV looks at the national picture, searching out the origins of our anti-urban trends, the pre- and post-war slum clearance policies we adopted, the wider pressures on cities and our national economy that fuel polarisation and abandonment, and attempts at regeneration and neighbourhood renewal.

- Part V draws together the lessons from the detailed study and the wider experience of urban problems in order to uncover and assemble current ideas about an urban renaissance that incorporates declining neighbourhoods.

Part I

Trends in two cities and four neighbourhoods

2 Method and approach

Our starting points for the report are:

- What drives neighbourhood decline? What are the symptoms? How long has it been going on?

- Which neighbourhoods experience acute decline? How widespread is the phenomenon?

- What measures are taken to prevent and cure the problems? Which ones work? Can neighbourhoods recover? Are some neighbourhoods doomed?

- What is the bigger picture? How do the worst areas fit into the general pattern of city and regional change?

Our work draws on two earlier studies funded by the Joseph Rowntree Foundation: *Swimming against the Tide*, a study of the 20 most difficult council estates over 15 years, and *Dangerous Disorder*, a study of 13 unpopular areas experiencing disorder and rioting in the early 1990s (Power and Tunstall, 1995, 1997). Both studies included Newcastle and Greater Manchester, but also covered much wider areas of the country. Many of the most unpopular estates were in London. In addition, we draw on the history of council housing (Power, 1987), two studies of European social housing (Power, 1995, 1997), and earlier work for the Department of Environment Priority Estates Project concerning unpopular areas in England and Wales (1979–89). We collected evidence of low demand from many parts of the country in the course of the work (see Appendices 1–3).

Our main focus is on Manchester and Newcastle, two cities experiencing long-run decline. Like other large cities, they are adversely hit both by the loss of key industries and by more general anti-urban trends. We choose these cities because the problems are clear, the impacts visible and the changes dramatic. The North is suffering most from the problems we are exploring. But we link our findings to the more general urban experience of low demand and exodus from certain neighbourhoods, coupled with changing demand for social housing.

We examine two neighbourhoods in each city. One shows acute symptoms of abandonment – streets with a majority of houses empty; demolition sites scattered throughout the area; empty property across the neighbourhood; property values falling; and intense demand problems in all property types, all tenures and all parts of the neighbourhood. The second neighbourhood is likewise in serious difficulty. But conditions generally have not plummeted to such a low point and there is more ground for hope that the situation can be stabilised or reversed. Each neighbourhood contains between 3,600 and 4,900 households, and represents either a single ward or adjacent parts of several wards. This size enabled us to cover all tenures and all services, but was small enough to understand in depth. Each ward was within a much larger, deprived area.

By adopting this approach, we aim to understand the problem on three levels – acute problems at city level; extreme problems at neighbourhood level; complete abandonment in the very worst pockets of the most difficult areas. The problems of these cities and neighbourhoods are not unique, but extreme, openly acknowledged. Their long roots are therefore traceable; also vigorous attempts are being made to do something about them. Thus, we can begin to understand the steepness of the decline; the political and community responses; and the potential for change.

We do not identify the neighbourhoods to avoid further negative images, though we acknowledge the invaluable help of many front-line staff and residents in the four areas. When reporting neighbourhood conditions, we number them M1, M2, N3, N4; M1 and M2 are in Manchester, N3 and N4 are in Newcastle. Those familiar with the actual scenes we describe will possibly recognise the specific areas, but their existing knowledge of the problems prevents further damage resulting from our work. Those concerned about the general problems of low demand and anxious to understand more fully what is going on do not need the exact location or names in order to appreciate the situation facing these neighbourhoods. The neighbourhoods share many characteristics with unpopular and difficult to manage urban areas all over the country, including in high demand cities like London. There is an intense hierarchy of popular and unpopular areas. The least popular suffer high levels of empty property, high turnover with some abandonment and demolition because of low demand (Hackney Borough Council, 1992; Southwark Council, 1994; Power and Tunstall, 1995).

It is possible to draw a broad distinction between low demand in economically prosperous cities and regions such as the South East and low demand in cities and regions suffering long-term structural decline such as the North. Throughout the report we make this distinction, although earlier work and research outside the North for this study suggest common patterns and pressures within cities

(DoE, 1981a). Our contention is that the economic decline, population loss and incipient abandonment evidenced in the North are a more extreme and therefore more visible manifestation of a wider process. The phenomenon also exists in most Northern European countries, though with distinct continental features and in different degrees (Caisse des Depots, 1998).

We drew on academic research in progress on this subject (Housing Corporation, 1997; Bramley, 1998; CIoH, 1998) and government research as well as earlier work (see Appendix 4 for full list).

We spoke to 104 staff in the following services: estate agents, voluntary bodies, shops, senior town hall officials, housing, regeneration, education, police, community work, social services, councillors and housing associations. We met with 24 residents' representatives in the four areas. Where possible, we met one senior and one front-line representative for each main service in each area (see Appendix 5 for breakdown by service). In addition, we interviewed local staff in other similar neighbourhoods. We spoke to a further 33 people across the country including chief executives, directors of housing and second tier officers.

Our aim in working close to the ground was to 'get under the skin of the problem'. In order to understand neighbourhood problems as fully as possible, we relied on four principal methods based on our experience of earlier neighbourhood investigations:

- direct observation of conditions and changes in conditions over time in the neighbourhoods

- direct interviews with the residents and staff living and working in a situation of acute decline

- collation of available facts on the areas from as wide a range of sources as possible including the Census, council reports and monitoring, government records and other research in the field

- interviews with senior officials responsible for neighbourhood strategies and interventions.

In addition, we collected press reports and local newsletters; we took photographs of the areas; we wrote observation notes immediately after every visit; we recorded and wrote up interviews; we documented empty sites and property; we mapped the smaller neighbourhoods within each area showing the tenure, the location of services, level of abandonment, progression of neighbourhood

emptying and changes to buildings.

We had not expected the problem to move so fast that, over the 16 months of our study, we would witness directly visible changes. However, there was a rapid progression over this short period both in the manifestation of the problem itself and in the approach to the problem by the cities. The people we spoke to left us with an urgent sense that their struggle to survive in such a vortex had been 'kept quiet for too long'. Therefore, whenever possible, we use their own words to convey the full force of events and to illustrate the issues we found wider evidence to support. No individual quote is directly attributed, but we make it clear which source we are using. We use individual quotations to support wider evidence, not as evidence in itself. We tried to avoid bias by checking all the case studies and quotations with local sources.

3 Changes in the two cities and four neighbourhoods

Below, we present demographic and economic evidence, comparing Manchester and Newcastle with the national picture. Where possible, we show comparable trends in the four neighbourhoods.

Population

Newcastle and Manchester were both much larger cities at the turn of the century than today (Halsey, 1988). Both have continued to lose population into the 1990s, but the rate of loss has slowed down and may stabilise or even reverse over the next few years. People in employment have moved out faster and further than jobs (DoE, 1996). Table 1 shows the population trend.

Outer areas have been depopulating too, though more slowly than inner areas. Table 2 shows this.

Table 3 shows the greater population losses in the four neighbourhoods.

The two Manchester neighbourhoods lost over one-third of their populations in the 1970s because of slum clearance. The Newcastle neighbourhoods experienced continuous serious decline over the whole period. The changes result in a fairly static supply of houses alongside declining population.

In spite of acute population losses, the number of households grew in both cities between 1981 and 1991 – by 3 per cent in Manchester and 6 per cent in Newcastle. To some extent, household formation is

Table 1 Population of cities of Manchester and Newcastle, 1971–96

Year	Manchester[1]	% change	Newcastle[2]	% change
1971	553,600		299,664	
1981	462,600		269,233	
1971–81		−16		−10
1991	438,500		255,985	
1981–91		−5		−5
1996	430,800		251,800	
1991–96		−2		−2
Population loss				
1971–96	−122,800	−22	−47,864	−16

Source: Manchester Committee Report, 30 May 1996; Manchester's 1996 Local Census; Newcastle City Profiles, 1997.

1 The figures for Manchester show the mid-year estimates prepared by the Registrar General in order to overcome the problem of the 1991 Census having largely excluded students.

2 The figures for Newcastle represent the private household population and exclude the institutional population. Newcastle City Council found that the mid-year estimate for 1996 over-compensated for under-enumeration in the 1991 Census, so Newcastle's own figures, based on their 1996 inter-censal survey together with the 1971, 1981 and 1991 Censuses, have been used here.

encouraged by available space. But, in the two Newcastle neighbourhoods, the absolute number of households shrank, suggesting extreme low demand.

Table 4 shows changes in the number of households in two cities and four neighbourhoods between 1981 and 1991.

Table 2 Population change in inner and outer areas of Manchester and Newcastle, 1971–91 (%)

	Manchester	Newcastle
1971–81		
Inner	–19	–21
Outer	–17	–7
1981–91		
Inner	–10	–8
Outer	–2	–3

Source: *Urban Trends in England* (DoE, 1996, p. 24).

Table 3 Population change in four inner areas and two cities, 1971–96 (%)

	Manchester	Newcastle	M1	M2	N3	N4
1971–81	–16	–10	–39	–39	–13	–15
1981–91	–5	–5	–5	–8	–19	–21
1991–96	–2	–2	–6	–7	–20	–10

Sources: 1981 and 1991 Census; Newcastle City Profiles, 1997; Manchester's 1996 Local Census.

Table 4 Changes in the number of households in two cities and four neighbourhoods, 1981–91 (%)

	Manchester	Newcastle	M1	M2	N3	N4
1981–91	+3	+6	+13	+3	–5	–9

Sources: Manchester Committee Report, 30 May 1996, based on the 1991 Census; Newcastle City Profiles, 1997, based on the 1991 Census.

Table 5 Population densities (residents per hectare)

Location		Neighbourhoods	
Great Britain	2.4		
England	3.6		
Inner London	78.1		
Greater London	42.3		
Birmingham	36.2		
Glasgow	33.1		
Manchester	34.9	M1 31	M2 37
Newcastle	23.2	N3 44	N4 42

Source: 1991 Census.

Table 6 Declining population of conurbations in thousands

Region	1961	1971	1981	1991	2001 (projected)
Greater Manchester	2,710	2,750	2,619	2,571	2,560
Tyne and Wear	1,241	1,218	1,155	1,130	1,114
Merseyside	1,711	1,662	1,522	1,450	1,386
Greater London	7,977	7,529	6,806	6,890	7,215

Sources: Annual Abstract of Statistics, 1998; PPI population estimates, 1998; 1996 based sub-national projection (PP3 98/1).

Density

Both cities have low population densities, less than half the density of inner London. While the overall population density of Britain is among the highest in Europe, urban densities generally are low (*Economist*, 1998). Paris, Madrid, Rome, Berlin are visibly more densely built up than London, for example. Table 5 shows the number of residents per hectare in the two cities and four neighbourhoods in comparison with other cities and nationally.

Table 6 highlights the long-running decline of urban areas leading to ever lower densities within the main cities of England. The Office of National Statistics (ONS) expects the overall decline of conurbations to continue, with the exception of Greater London, based on the 1996 population figures (ONS, 1998).

Jobs

The population and density changes are mirrored by job changes. The figures comparing 1984 and 1991 show that jobs in inner areas continued to disappear while jobs in the outer areas grew. In outer Manchester, jobs expanded by 41 per cent. Table 7 shows this. The increase in outer city jobs contrasts with outer population decline.

The pattern of jobs has changed radically with the losses heavily concentrated among male workers and the gains among females. Table 8 shows this.

The starkest losses were in manufacturing, as shown in Table 9.

The surprisingly large increase in public service jobs in Newcastle may be due in part to specific boundaries, to the relocation of government offices to Newcastle, and to the fact that the definition of 'public services' includes health care provided by the private sector, for example. Manchester City lost public service jobs, whilst the rest of the Greater Manchester conurbation gained 55,000 (an increase of 44 per cent) (Turok and Edge, forthcoming).

The proportion of the population unemployed (registered for work but without a job) was more than double the national average in the two cities, but much higher in the four inner areas than in the cities as a whole. Table 10 shows the unemployment rates between 1991 and 1996/97. Unemployment dropped significantly over the five years from 1991 in the two Manchester areas but rose in the Newcastle areas. Mirroring the general job changes, unemployment dropped far more rapidly for women than for men.

The proportion of the working age population *not* in work or studying is far higher in both cities and nationally than the recorded unemployment rate; in the four inner areas almost half the population of working age is outside the labour market and education (see Table 11). This problem has got worse.

Table 7 Employment change in Manchester and Newcastle, 1984–91 (% total jobs)

	Manchester	Newcastle
Inner	–6	–7
Outer	+41	+9

Source: *Urban Trends in England* (DoE, 1996, p. 44).

Table 8 Employment change for male and female workers in inner and outer areas of Manchester and Newcastle, 1984–91 (as a % of full-time equivalents)

	Manchester		Newcastle	
	Male	Female	Male	Female
Inner	–13	+1	–19	+4
Outer*	+25	+54	–1	+14

Source: *Urban Trends in England* (DoE, 1996, p. 44).

* Outer Manchester is a small proportion of the city as a whole, making the % changes more extreme

Table 9 Changes in sector of employment in the cities of Manchester and Newcastle, 1981–96

	Great Britain (%)		Manchester (%)		Newcastle (%)	
Manufacturing	–1,950,000	(–33)	–38,600	(–62)	–12,700	(–42)
Private services	+2,899,000	(+35)	–2,750	(–2)	+1,200	(+1)
Public services	+ 988,000	(+22)	–5,250	(–7)	+14,500	(+35)

Sources: Annual Employment Survey/Census of Employment; Turok and Edge (forthcoming).

Notes: See notes at end of Chapter 3.

Table 10 Male and female unemployment rate, 1991–96/97 (%)

		Nationally	Manchester	Newcastle[1]	M1	M2	N3	N4
1991[1]	Male	11	23	19	29	32	35	38
	Female	7	14	10	19	16	18	19
1997[2]	Male	8	17	21*	19	23	39*	43*
	Female	3	6	9*	5	5	13*	16*

Sources: Newcastle City Profiles, 1991; Newcastle City Profiles, 1996; Social Trends, 1998; Manchester Ward Profiles, 1991; *Manchester Matters*, 1997; Census, 1991.

1 1991 figures represent Census unemployment rates. Newcastle's 1996 (*) figures are also based on Census unemployment rates.

2 1997 figures are based on the Office of National Statistics claimant counts. This may lower the Manchester figures.

Table 11 Percentage of working age population not in work or studying or training, 1991

National	Manchester	Newcastle	M1	M2	N3	N4
24	37	31	46	48	49	50

Source: 1991 Census.

Notes to Table 9

- These figures treat full-time jobs as equivalent to part-time posts, thereby ignoring the shift from the former to the latter.

- The Annual Employment Survey/Census of Employment does not record self-employment, which increased over the period.

- Manchester and Newcastle are defined as the City Council areas in both cases, not wider conurbations whose definition is more ambiguous. The outer conurbations of most cities performed better than the cores over the period 1981–96 (interestingly, Leeds and Newcastle were the two exceptions).

- Occupational data (e.g. manual/non-manual) are available only from the Census of Population. Considerable manipulation is required to identify the changes between 1981 and 1991 since definitions changed over this period. However, the bulk of manual jobs tend to be in manufacturing industry, so its decline is a good indicator of the loss of manual jobs. Some manual jobs are also found in two service sectors: (i) distribution, hotels and catering (mainly unskilled); and (ii) transport and communications (mainly skilled). Both sectors declined in Newcastle between 1981–96. Distribution, etc. also declined in Manchester, but transport and communications expanded slightly.

Source: Ivan Turok.

4 Social dynamics

In the following sections, we examine some of the social problems common to urban areas.

Deprivation

Based on the Government's new index of local deprivation (DETR, 1998a), Manchester ranks as the third most deprived area in England and Newcastle 19th, out of 354. Although Manchester scores higher on most indicators than Newcastle, both score higher than all their surrounding authorities. Table 12 shows this.

Table 13 shows the 20 most deprived local authority areas. Newcastle is less than five points behind Islington at tenth, which is only four points behind Manchester at third. Inner London and the Midlands rank among the most deprived areas of the country. This underlines the national dimension of concentrated deprivation. On core indices, the most deprived boroughs and neighbourhoods show similar patterns, though the intensity of specific problems varies.

Table 12 Degree of deprivation on 12 indicators in local authorities around Greater Manchester and Tyneside

| Authority | Degree of deprivation | |
	Deprivation score	Rank among local authorities
Manchester	36.33	3
Salford	26.64	23
Rochdale	25.13	29
Oldham	24.82	33
Bolton	20.66	47
Tameside	19.78	53
Trafford	7.42	129
Stockport	3.81	177
Newcastle	27.95	19
Sunderland	26.90	21
Gateshead	24.58	35
South Tyneside	23.67	38
North Tyneside	18.67	62

Source: DETR, 1998a.

Table 13 The top 20 local authorities on the government's new index of deprivation in rank order

	Area	Score
1	Liverpool	40.07
2	Newham	38.55
3	Manchester	36.33
4	Hackney	35.21
5	Birmingham	34.67
6	Tower Hamlets	34.30
7	Sandwell	33.78
8	Southwark	33.74
9	Knowsley	33.69
10	Islington	32.21
11	Greenwich	31.58
12	Lambeth	31.57
13	Haringey	31.53
14	Lewisham	29.44
15	Barking and Dagenham	28.69
16	Nottingham	28.44
17	Camden	28.23
18	Hammersmith and Fulham	28.19
19	Newcastle upon Tyne	27.95
20	Brent	26.95

Source: DETR, 1998a.

Concentrated deprivation

Table 14 shows the proportion of households experiencing deprivation, long-term unemployment, in manual rather than non-manual jobs, and children in lone parent households. Manual work is associated with lower pay and job losses; lone parenthood is associated with poverty and other risks (Kiernan, 1997; Hobcraft, 1998; Gregg, forthcoming)

A large majority of male workers in the four areas class themselves as manual workers, far above the national or city averages. Jobs have changed but the skills of the male population have not changed at the same rate.

There is a surplus of men with a manual work background, a loss of manual jobs (particularly from inner cities), coupled with a rise in female employment, more often in non-manual, service occupations. Our neighbourhoods fare particularly badly because of their history of industrial, low skill, working class employment. Concentrated poverty was, according to reports from both cities, the single biggest explanatory factor in neighbourhood problems (Manchester and Newcastle, 1998).

The four wards we studied come within the 5 per cent most deprived wards in England. All the neighbourhoods are part of a wider area of severe deprivation. Mapping the 5 per cent most deprived wards in England (on both Breadline Britain and work poverty indices) shows large 'poverty clusters' (CASE, 1998). In Manchester, 16 wards, including our two neighbourhoods, form one poverty cluster. In Newcastle, one neighbourhood is in a cluster of four wards, the other in a cluster of three wards (see Table 15).

Table 14 Characteristics of city and neighbourhood populations

		Nationally	Manchester	Newcastle	M1	M2	N3	N4
Households deprived[1] (%)		18	34	30	41	41	39	46
Long-term unemployed (% of all unemployed), July 1997 (* January 1998)		27*	39	34*	40	38	45	42
Manual, 1991[2]	All	41	48	42	66	62	61	67
(% of all employed)	Men only	49	56	50	73	70	76	82
Children in lone parent households[3] (%)		11	37	32	39	35	33	33

Source: Labour Force Survey, 1990 and 1991; 1991 Census; Newcastle's 1996 Inter-Censal Survey; Regional Trends, 1998; *Manchester Matters*, 1997; Newcastle City Council Community Appraisal, 1997.

1 As defined in Breadline Britain index.

2 Includes the following socio-economic groups from the 1991 Census: manual workers (foremen, supervisors, skilled and own account), personal service and semi-skilled manual workers, unskilled manual workers.

3 As defined in 1991 Census.

Table 15 Poverty clusters

Neighbourhood	No. of wards in cluster	Population of cluster[1]
M1+M2	16	175,000
N3	4	35,000
N4	3	27,000

Source: CASE, 1998.

1 Population figures from 1991 Census.

Ethnic composition

Manchester has a high concentration of ethnic minority households compared with Newcastle and the country as a whole, with 13 per cent of the population belonging to ethnic minority groups. Newcastle is below the national average with 4 per cent. Ethnic minorities are under-represented in all four inner areas we studied. Ninety-five per cent of their populations or more are classed as white. Table 16 shows this.

This distribution reflects the fact that the four inner areas were all traditional working class neighbourhoods linked to the heavy manufacturing of their earlier growth eras. The predominantly white character of the four areas underlines a finding from earlier work on riots and on marginal estates that race is not a cause of acute urban decline, though it may become part of the process in areas where large numbers of ethnic minority households live (Power, 1997; Power and Tunstall, 1997; Modood et al., 1997).

Crime

National and city crime levels between 1993 and 1997 fell steadily. But violent crime rose in England and more steeply in Manchester. Figures for Northumbria, including Newcastle, show a significant fall in all crime, including violent crime. Table 17 shows this.

In all our neighbourhoods, crime, harassment and witness intimidation are big problems. Drug use and drug dealing were frequently mentioned. We found a high consciousness of crime, and the areas have all had high-profile press coverage of particularly serious incidents. But special measures, particularly by the police, housing service and residents, have had a strong, positive impact. Proactive policing had made significant in-roads into hard-core crime, and co-ordinated action with residents had increased confidence and quality of life.

As a result, one of the neighbourhoods has a burglary rate below the city average. Fewer than one in five feels unsafe in this area. This compares with nearly one in two feeling unsafe in another area, although reported crime there has reduced by 50 per cent over the past six

Table 16 Ethnic composition of Manchester, Newcastle and four areas, 1991 (%)

	National average	Cities		Areas			
		Manchester	Newcastle	M1	M2	N3	N4
White	94.5	87	96	96	95	98	99
Non-white	5.5	13	4	4	5	2	1

Sources: Census, 1991; DoE, 1996.

years as Figure 1 illustrates (Newcastle City Council, 1994; Northumbria Police, 1998). Although there is often a problem of under-reporting, the active police presence in these areas, including witness support, and the good working relationship between police, housing staff and residents, helps explain the fall.

Table 17 Notifiable offences recorded by the police per 100,000 population by police force area and offence group

Police force area	Year	All crimes	Violent crime	Burglary	Theft and handling
England	1993	10,846	575	2,703	5,410
	1994	10,296	610	2,480	5,014
	1995	9,960	607	2,420	4,706
	1996	9,795	667	2,275	4,643
	1997	8,885	666	1,973	4,195
Greater Manchester	1993	14,178	654	3,802	6,831
	1994	13,111	615	3,532	6,023
	1995	12,723	622	3,330	5,797
	1996	12,721	727	3,249	5,620
	1997	11,936	847	2,944	5,168
Northumbria	1993	14,840	576	4,371	6,119
	1994	14,120	564	3,959	5,689
	1995	13,466	546	3,667	5,468
	1996	11,796	497	2,977	4,776
	1997	9,770	453	2,411	4,209

Source: *Criminal Statistics England and Wales*. London: HMSO, 1993–97.

Figure 1 Total recorded crimes in neighbourhood (N3) 1992–98

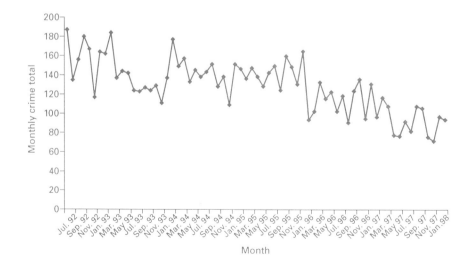

5 Housing patterns – how problematic are they?

Next we examine housing patterns to establish their effect on the overall decline of the cities and neighbourhoods.

Tenure

The way housing is owned in the two cities is very different from the national pattern, though it is fairly typical of inner urban areas. Table 18 shows the tenure pattern.

Both Manchester and Newcastle have nearly double the national proportion of council stock and more housing association activity than average. Conversely, they have far lower levels of owner occupation and around the average for private renting. The tenure distribution is even more skewed in the four neighbourhoods with a higher proportion of social renting than the city average –at least two-and-a-half times the national level. A majority of all housing in the neighbourhoods is council owned. Owner occupation is less than half the national average.

The relatively low level of owner occupation in the cities as a whole and the four neighbourhoods in particular has an impact on who lives in the city, who leaves and who wants to stay. In predominantly low income neighbourhoods within significantly low income cities, tenure plays a very important role – originally in ensuring that the poor were housed, but today driving depopulation as the numbers wanting and able to buy have risen, particularly in younger age groups. But, if the neighbourhood conditions are poor, then few will want to invest in owner occupation even if it is available and cheap, thus fuelling a vicious circle, as illustrated in Figure 2.

People leave for surrounding areas, such as North Tyneside outside Newcastle, or Rochdale and Altrincham, outside Manchester. This pattern has resulted in low Right to Buy levels, far below the national average. Owner occupiers already in these neighbourhoods often 'feel completely trapped' by declining property values, and the surrounding social and environmental problems (Manchester City Council, 1998e).

Housing associations are significant providers of rented housing in the cities and neighbourhoods. Their role in regeneration has

Table 18 The tenure pattern in the two cities and four neighbourhoods, compared with the national average (%)

	National average	Manchester	Newcastle	M1	M2	N3	N4
Local authority renting	20	38	35	50	54	48	77
Owner occupied	68	41	50	28	30	35	16
Private renting	9	12	9	8	8	10	2
Housing associations	3	7	5	13	6	6	4

Source: 1991 Census (from Newcastle City Profiles and Manchester Ward Profiles); ONS *et al.* (1996).

Figure 2 Vicious circle of tenure and conditions in low income neighbourhoods

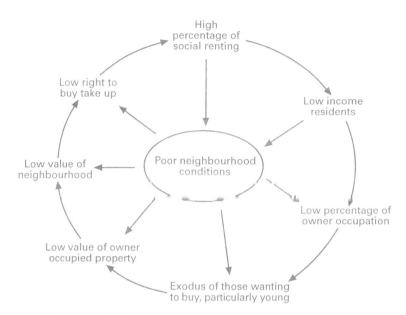

Source: Manchester and Newcastle, 1998.

led to their strong growth in the 1990s.

The private rented sector is small. The high proportion of social renting – two-thirds of all households – helps to explain this. Nonetheless, private landlords let often to marginal households. The local authorities saw private landlords as offering a fail-safe for people. They play an important role within the cities and local authorities want to involve them in neighbourhood renewal (Manchester and Newcastle, 1998). The case studies suggest a growth in private renting since 1991.

Changing housing patterns

Tenure change in the two cities has followed national trends, with a rise in owner occupation, a fall in council renting and a rise in housing association renting. In the neighbourhoods, the increase in housing association property was

conspicuous, even though, as a proportion of total households, the sector remained small. In neighbourhood N4, for example, although the point change was relatively small, the actual number of households living in the housing association sector more than tripled and those in owner occupation doubled. Other changes were generally smaller than average (see Table 19).

Many of the council losses in the cities were to Right to Buy purchasers. Some of these purchasers later became private landlords when they could not sell on their properties. But, in all the neighbourhoods, there was very little Right to Buy. Table 20 shows the proportion of sales in both cities and the four neighbourhoods.

Figure 3 shows the proportion of council stock that has been sold across 26 wards in Newcastle, varying from nearly 50 per cent to under 5 per cent. Our two neighbourhoods are close to the bottom.

Table 19 Tenure change as a % point change of share of total, 1981–91

	National average	Manchester	Newcastle	M1	M2	N3	N4
Local authority	−10	−9	−11	−7	−3	−7	−12
Owner occupation	+11	+5	+11	+2	0	+3	+9
Private rented	−2	+1[1]	−2	−2[1]	0[1]	−1	−1
Housing association	+1	+2	+2	+7	+3	+4	+3

Source: 1991 and 1981 Census data collated by Manchester and Newcastle City Council; ONS *et al.* (1996).

1 A small number of properties rented with a job or business have been included in the private rented figures for 1991. These were previously included in the housing association figures.

Table 20 Levels of Right to Buy sales, 1981–98

	National average	Manchester	Newcastle	M1	M2	N3	N4
Percentage of 1981 stock sold to sitting tenants	25	14	19	8[1]	2[1]	3	9

Source: City Councils, 1998.

1 Percentage of 1998 stock.

Figure 3 The pattern of Right to Buy sales in Newcastle showing the percentage of stock sold in each ward

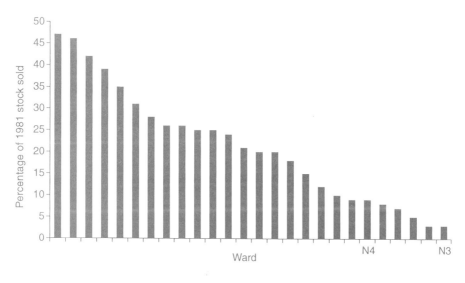

Source: Newcastle City Council, June 1998.

Housing types

The two cities have a high proportion of houses – around 70 per cent of the stock. Flats are concentrated in post-war council estates, some older pre-war blocks, sub-divided older houses and Tyneside flats. A majority of the houses are terraced and many date from the nineteenth century. A tiny proportion are detached.

The four neighbourhoods are also predominantly made up of houses, mainly terraced. Terraced houses are both Victorian and council-built in this century. Terraced houses have been traditionally popular across the country but, in all four neighbourhoods, the back alleys and yards between properties, built for soil carts to remove sewage before modern drains, led to abandonment (see photographs).

Table 21 shows the break-down of housing types.

Generally, the housing stock in all four neighbourhoods is attractive, solidly built, well laid out and well maintained. Even semi-abandoned streets are generally made up of such property. There are only one or two estates and blocks of clumsy, unattractive design. Many of the least popular, hardest to manage blocks have been demolished. Overall it is hard to see physical housing design or quality reasons why these neighbourhoods have hit such extreme difficulty. The photographs show this.

Table 21 The distribution of types of stock in the two cities and four neighbourhoods (percentage)

Stock type	National average	Manchester	Newcastle	M1	M2	N3	N4
Detached	22	3	5	1	1	2	1
Semi-detached	31	28	31	22	10	32	10
Terraced	28	41	32	56	59	46	53
Flat	19	28	32	21	30	21	37

Sources: *Social Trends* (ONS, 1997, p. 172); 1991 Census (quoted in Manchester Ward Profiles and Newcastle City Profiles).

Back alleys

High quality modern housing association property in low demand

Housing association properties – empties and occupied homes are interspersed

Part II
Evidence of incipient abandonment

6 Urban abandonment

Next, we look at evidence from the four neighbourhoods of actual abandonment. Abandonment signals the loss of value and use of an area. It attracts vandalism, boarding up and neglect of conditions. It often leads to arson, crime and refuse dumping. It lowers standards more generally and creates fear. The starkest measure of an area's decline is visible empty property (Power, 1987, 1997; Downes, 1989).

The four neighbourhoods experienced a build-up of abandoned homes, either with net curtains to disguise their emptiness or with steel, sytex or wooden security shuttering. In all of the areas, whole streets and groups of streets were semi-abandoned.

Empty property

In the four neighbourhoods, the picture is complex and sometimes out of control. The Newcastle neighbourhoods have between 13 and 20 per cent of their council property empty. The Manchester areas have risen steeply from 5 per cent two years ago to around 15 per cent. The problem of abandonment in Manchester is believed to be catching up with Newcastle (Manchester City Council, 1998e). Both cities reported a swift, sudden and unexpected loss of demand. We counted the numbers of empty properties in specific streets in the worst affected areas on a specific day. Table 22 summarises what we found in particular streets. This exercise does *not* show the overall pattern of empty property in the four neighbourhoods. Appendix 9 shows city-wide levels of empty property in the private and public sectors, difficult to let properties and demolition figures.

We observed the following in the worst affected areas:

- The boarded up properties can belong to the local authority, a local housing association, a private landlord, an owner occupier – abandonment is affecting all tenures.

- The semi-abandoned streets or blocks include Victorian terraces, 1930s council cottages, post-war houses, modern housing association developments less than ten years old, small blocks of sheltered flats, 1960s' and 1970s' purpose-built estates – all property types are involved.

- The streets with boarded up properties are not on the whole badly maintained, or unappealing; they tend to contain attractive, small-scale, well built houses with gardens; transferred to an inner London context, many of the properties would be gentrified.

- There are frequent discussions in the city councils about demolition – the de-stabilising effect on the community is intense.

- Some unlet properties belonging to housing associations are in pristine condition; they cost around £60,000 a unit to build less than ten years ago – their abandonment is hard to explain.

- Some Victorian terraces are solid, attractive and renovated, but the backs are a jumble of outhouses, high walls and rubbish-strewn alleys – ugly, insecure and long outdated. No way has been found of turning these yards and alleys into secure, joined-up back gardens.

- Many individual houses are still attractive but the neighbourhood environment is an active deterrent.

Many managers and residents believe that there simply are not enough people to keep the houses filled. The people have gone but the houses are there and, in one or two places, are still being built!

Table 22 The tenure, number of units and volume of empty property in 30 streets in four neighbourhoods on a specific day in 1998

Street or block	Tenure (main landlord)	No. of units	No. empty	% empty
1	Local authority	6	5	83
2	Local authority	208	93	45
3	Local authority	34	14	41
4	Local authority	60	17	28
5	Local authority	27	7	26
6	Local authority	16	4	25
7	Local authority	90	22	24
8	Local authority	63	13	21
9	Local authority	90	19	21
10	Local authority	16	3	19
11	Local authority	37	7	19
12	Local authority	90	15	17
13	Local authority	27	4	15
14	Local authority	111	14	13
15	Local authority	50	6	12
16	Local authority	94	11	12
17	Local authority	87	7	8
18	Local authority	171	11	6
19	Housing association/private	11	7	64
20	Housing association/private	74	47	64
21	Housing association/private	26	15	58
22	Housing association/private	12	6	50
23	Housing association/private	82	32	39
24	Housing association/private	84	30	36
25	Housing association/private	55	18	33
26	Housing association/private	26	8	31
27	Private	12	6	50
28	Private	37	15	40
29	Private	24	5	20
30	Private	26	5	19

Source: Fieldwork street counts and LA Housing Department information, September 1998.

This emptying street is likely to be demolished (private and HA)

Demolition

In each city, there is now a regular demolition programme of at least 250 local authority properties a year. It is likely to rise based on current predictions. These figures do not include the much larger-scale demolition within regeneration programmes in all four neighbourhoods. They also do not include private demolitions which are significant, but not monitored in the same way by the local authority. The demolitions keep the volume of empty homes within bounds in the worst hit areas. However, three of the four neighbourhoods appear to be experiencing galloping abandonment in restricted areas.

Demolition has not generally stemmed the tide of abandonment although demolition of specific unpopular blocks has sometimes increased the popularity of surrounding houses. In some instances, demolition has fuelled the problem, creating an atmosphere of uncertainty over the future of the area, giving a signal of zero value and zero demand, thereby deterring would-be applicants. Many demolition decisions are being made in response to immediate neighbourhood conditions without a clear overall plan, or a full option appraisal (Newcastle City Council, 1998b). Other nearby streets then often start to show the same symptoms, as the blight from abandonment infects the atmosphere of the surrounding streets and fear drives people in adjacent streets away.

Views about demolition were very mixed with most people seeing it as both positive and negative. Some current demolition proposals are provoking objections and there is certainly not unanimous support for it, even where levels of abandonment are high. Remaining residents often want to hold on (see Part IV). While demolition helped remove blighted property, it signalled a more general loss of confidence in the area when the demolished property was sound and in good condition, as it usually was.

Other cities are demolishing council housing on a larger scale: 2,000 council homes a year are being demolished in Glasgow (Webster, 1998); at least 8,000 council properties were demolished in Liverpool in the 1980s, only a small proportion of which were replaced (Ridley, 1996). There is also significant council demolition going on in London, based on regeneration schemes in the 1990s – for example, in Hackney 5,000, Southwark 2,000, Tower Hamlets 2,000, Brent 3,000 and Islington 600. The particular problems of the two cities we studied closely are part of a much bigger process. However, central government and regional offices do not have up-to-date information on the scale of demolition (DETR, 1997a).

Pace of abandonment

The speed with which streets or blocks are shifting from being relatively well occupied to nearly half-empty is alarming. Over a relatively long period, the level of turnover had been unusually high; new demand was heavily concentrated among more transient, unstable and younger households; and the level of empty property was above the city average of 3–5 per cent – at least 15 per cent in two of the neighbourhoods. This created instability and a reduction in informal social controls leaving a vacuum which eventually tipped a highly localised low demand area into rapid abandonment. Table 23 shows the rapid change.

Table 23 Empty council property in the four neighbourhoods over the period 1995–98

| Year | Neighbourhood levels of empty property (number of empties) | | | |
	M1	M2	N3	N4
1995–96 (quarter 4)	81	43	260	308
1996–97 (quarter 4)	127	148	257	309
1997–98 (quarter 1)	176	174	244	341
1997–98 (quarter 2)	231	230	214	344
1997–98 (quarter 3)	211	238	217	417
1997–98 (quarter 4)	260	234	225	424
1998–99 (quarter 1)	326	277	252	442
1998–99 (quarter 2)	317	306	215[1]	473

Source: Newcastle and Manchester Housing Departments.

1 Demolitions account for the different pattern of empty property in this neighbourhood.

Table 24 highlights the change on specific estates or in small areas within the neighbourhoods.

Property values

Low property values reflect the reducing economic and social value of these areas. In some pockets of all four areas, some owner occupied property cannot be sold at all. We found private properties that had been bought for £30,000 seven years ago now worth only £5,000, and properties bought for £20,000 ten years ago worth only £2,000. The low private property values help explain the low level of Right to Buy in the areas. The discounted value of Right to Buy – around £13,000 – was only a little below the national average of £15,000, but far above the private market value (see Table 25).

Table 24 The rapid change in % of empty property in six small areas within the four neighbourhoods, 1995–98

	1995–96	1996–97	1997–98
Small area 1	2	6	19
Small area 2	7	13	16
Small area 3	6	18	35
Small area 4	4	8	15
Small area 5 9% (1993)	13	14	15
Small area 6 5% (1994)	12	13	18

Source: Newcastle and Manchester Housing Departments.

Table 25 Right to Buy values (after discount)

	Neighbourhood 1	Neighbourhood 2
Manchester	£16,250	£10,170
Newcastle	£11,500	£14,700

Source: City Councils.

Note: National average £15,000.

An estate agent in one of the areas explained the problem in these words:

I have been an estate agent practising in the inner city for the past 23 years. In the last five years, property prices in these areas have slumped, in my opinion due to the fact that a large amount of crime and vandalism has been rife within these areas. If the properties are empty, then they will be vandalised within hours of the former occupants leaving the property. Anything of value such as combination boilers and pipework, fires, kitchen units and bathroom units are immediately stripped from the properties and sold.

People will no longer tolerate living in the inner city areas and there has been a massive breakdown in the communities due to the fact that properties are broken into on a regular basis, owners threatened and I know of cases personally where owner occupiers have moved out and given their properties up for possession because they have been threatened by local gangs of thugs.

The estate agent gave some current examples of the changes in private property values in one of our neighbourhoods (see Table 26).

Turnover and access to council housing

Turnover counts numbers leaving in a year as a proportion of occupied units at the beginning. We have turnover figures only for the local authority stock. But, when we spoke to residents and landlords, we understood turnover to be a serious problem in all tenures. The figures suggest extraordinarily high turnover rates within the council stock. Both cities far exceed the national average turnover across their council stock (see Table 27).

In spite of the loss of one-quarter of the national council stock under Right to Buy, transfer of ownership to other landlords and demolitions, social landlords continued to allocate over a quarter of a million properties in each year from 1979 to new tenants. By 1995, the overall volume of social lettings rose

Table 26 Examples of falling private property values in one neighbourhood

	Previous value		1998 value
Property 1	£23,995	(1991)	No value
Property 2	£28,000	(1989/90)	£5,000
Property 3	£28,000	(1990)	£5,000

Source: Estate agent's information provided to private sector team, Manchester, 1998.

Table 27 Rate of reletting[1] in council housing in the two cities and nationally, 1996/97 (%)

National	Manchester	Newcastle
12.5	19.5	22.4

Source: HIP1 returns to the DETR, 1997.

1 These figures represent the total lettings divided by the total dwellings, as recorded on the HIP1 forms.

significantly, as Figure 4 shows, although the large increase in housing association new lets drew some tenants out of council housing.

A significant proportion of vacancies are due to the more elderly tenant population dying off (Burrows, 1997). Therefore, within council housing, increasingly youthful households have been rehoused at a surprisingly high rate. The rate of turnover also reflects increasing choice, which in itself can be seen as positive, and high turnover areas have always played a role in cities. But, if turnover moves above a certain level, it can become unmanageable. Across the neighbourhoods, the turnover rate was between 20 and 50 per cent. Table 28 illustrates the problem.

Waiting lists

Local authority waiting lists are not a reliable predictor of demand. About 40 per cent of applicants disappear each year through finding other housing solutions, changing plans, circumstances and aspirations (Prescott-Clark *et al.*, 1994). Nor are waiting lists sensitive to the restricted options which many applicants are willing to contemplate. Applicants have little

Figure 4 Volume of lettings to new tenants by social landlords, 1979–95

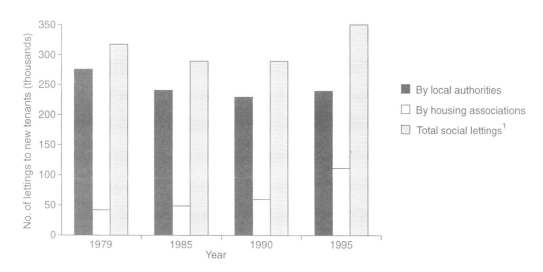

Source: Hills in Glennerster and Hills (1998, p. 156).

1 There may be a small amount of double-counting as a result of housing associations sometimes allocating to council tenants.

Table 28 Level of turnover in 16 specific estates or areas of council housing, 1996–97

Estate or block	Neighbourhood	Number of units	Turnover % per annum (1996/97)
1	M1	366	24
2	M1	300	20
3	M1	405	40
4	M1	96	54
5	M1	293	25
6	M1	199	30
7	M2	182	28
8	M2	300	20
9	M2	225	23
10	N3	470	29
11	N3	540	34
12	N3	398	36
13	N4	196	51
14	N4	115	47
15	N4	87	46
16	N4	127	54

Source: Manchester and Newcastle housing departments, 1997.

Table 29 Numbers on the waiting list for Manchester and Newcastle, 1992–1997

	1992	1993	1994	1995	1996	1997
Manchester	17,395[3]	12,743	9,507	8,564	6,149	5,318[2]
% of stock[1]	24	18	14	13	9	8
Newcastle	5,531	5,694	5,393	5,203	4,812	4,508[2]
% of stock[1]	13	14	13.5	13	12	12

Sources: Newcastle City Council Housing Annual Reports 1992–97; Manchester Committee Report, 30 May 1996; and Manchester Housing Department, 1998.

1 Stock figures from DETR.

2 Estimated numbers leaving council stock each year: Manchester, 11,500; Newcastle, 3,800.

3 According to Manchester, this figure may include transfers. All others do not.

Table 30 Numbers on the waiting list for
Newcastle, 1986–91

	1986	1987	1988	1989	1991
Newcastle	12,500	7,542	5,721	5,209	5,372

Source: Newcastle City Council Housing
Annual Reports, 1986–91

idea what they will be offered or when, though they can often state a broad area preference. The system is usually highly impersonal with little direct or proactive choice. Rehousing is generally based on some criterion of need. Therefore, only needy people generally apply. Refusal of offers is the main mechanism of 'choice'. Also many waiting lists, particularly for large urban authorities, are not up-to-date because of the scale of the council stock and the volume of turnover. Nonetheless, they do give some idea of general demand.

Newcastle's waiting list fell by 1,023 from 1992, while Manchester's fell by 12,000. Table 29 shows the exact figures.

The steep decline in Manchester's list since 1992 is mainly because of the council undertaking a major 'clean-up' of the list to ensure that those people registered do actually want housing. Manchester's exclusion policy for ineligible applicants accounts for only a small part of the overall reduction (Manchester City Council, 1998f).

In Newcastle, the steep decline occurred earlier: there was a significant drop between 1986 and 1987 explained by increased efficiency in monitoring the waiting list at this time. Since then, numbers have generally continued to fall, though more gradually. Table 30 shows this.

The waiting time to be rehoused had dropped in both cities. Table 31 based on Manchester's figures shows that a majority in the least popular neighbourhood are rehoused within a month of applying. In the less decayed neighbourhood, the wait is on average six months for a house, less for a flat. There are also popular areas in the cities with longer waiting times.

In both Newcastle neighbourhoods, we were told there was virtually no waiting list or waiting time for rehousing. Both cities have now opened their allocations and are advertising nationally.

Table 31 Demand for properties in the Manchester neighbourhoods – % of properties by waiting time
(based on expected turnover and actual numbers on the waiting list)

	Houses Waiting time in months			Low rise flats Waiting time in months		
	Less than 1	2–9	Over 9	Less than 1	2–9	Over 9
M1						
1996	53	46	2	88	5	7
1997	54	44	2	86	8	6
M2						
1996	31	38	30	52	15	34
1997	39	29	32	61	17	22

Source: Manchester City Council Housing Department.

 **Housing Department**

Property to Let

DETAILS:

RENTS RANGE
3 BEDROOM HOUSES FROM £30-£36 P/W
2 BEDROOM HOUSES FROM £32-£40 P/W

ALL EXCLUSIVE OF HOUSING BENEFIT

Features Include:

 GAS FIRED CENTRAL HEATING TO RADIATORS

 FITTED UNITS AND PLUMBING TO WASHING MACHINE TO KITCHENS

 AREA BENEFITS FROM PARTIAL C.C.T.V. SURVEILLANCE AND SECURITY PATROLS

 NEARBY SCHOOLS, SHOPS AND COMMUNITY FACILITIES

 LOCALLY BASED NEIGHBOURHOOD HOUSING OFFICE PROVIDING COMPREHENSIVE HOUSING
SERVICES

 NEARBY BUS SERVICE TO   CITY CENTRE

 RENTS SHOWN ARE EXCLUSIVE OF HOUSING BENEFIT

 CLOSE PROXIMITY TO RIVERSIDE WALKWAY

 'FURNITURE PACKAGES' AVAILABLE AT ADDITIONAL CHARGE

Housing associations

While council housing is dominant in the cities and neighbourhoods, housing associations have become increasingly important. They entered the scene in the 1970s, renovating older terraced property. In the 1980s, they became the favoured regeneration partners and implementers of government policy. Local authorities, government offices for the regions and politicians, afraid of losing 'their share of the cake', argued for the need to diversify tenure; create newer, higher quality housing; and capitalise on government support.

Because it was cheaper to develop in the North and jobs were short, many argued that the North should continue to receive its share of capital allocations for housing. The result is that some very attractive, small-scale, high quality developments tucked into the four areas are experiencing extreme low demand, either 'poaching' tenants from older but often renovated council housing or simply finding properties unlettable.

Housing associations have also actively bought up street properties from retreating owner occupiers as prices fell. But the common problem facing both kinds of social landlords is plummeting demand.

Some argue that attractive, new, small-scale developments enhance the prospects of regeneration and help to keep people in the area who otherwise might have moved away. The alternative view is that, unless job opportunities expand, such strategies are bound to fail.

Some residents actively campaigned against housing association development, whilst, in other parts, residents supported or even initiated development. But housing associations are now demolishing unlettable, unsellable property. Unless regeneration takes off, much of the costly building of the last ten years will be wasted.

Private landlords

Private renting began to make a comeback in the wake of deregulation and the collapse in the

Housing association sheltered scheme completed c. 1990 – likely to be demolished

Table 32 Level of empty property at 1997 in small areas within the neighbourhoods

	Units in area	Number of units empty	% empty
Housing associations			
HA1	183	99	54
HA2	16	9	56
HA3	282	144	51
Private landlords			
Area 1	329	138	42
Area 2	137	26	19
Area 3	447	134	30
Area 4	1,905	362	19
Area 5	24	12	50
Area 6	93	37	40
Area 7	120	24	20

Source: Interviews with housing associations and local authority statistics.

owner occupier market in the late 1980s (Malpass and Means, 1993).

Low income owners, unable to sell at a level that would redeem their mortgage, sometimes became landlords of last resort, using the housing benefit system. The same housing benefit incentive, until recently paying 100 per cent of the full rent for low income tenants, has attracted speculative private landlords too. There were rumours of various 'scams'. But private landlords are seriously affected by abandonment.

Table 32 shows the level of empty property experienced by housing associations and private landlords in small areas within the neighbourhoods.

Rented housing in all sectors was experiencing a serious collapse in demand:

- structurally sound, attractive, improved properties proved unlettable

- weak social controls and high levels of vandalism led to empty properties often being destroyed

- social landlords were operating in direct competition with each other

- landlords and tenants used the '100% benefit system' to facilitate the movement of a diminishing number of tenants around surplus stock

- private landlords speculated around demolition decisions, buying up property for little in the hope of high rent from temporary lettings, before Compulsory Purchase Orders

- private landlords were often willing to rehouse evicted tenants as long as the rent was guaranteed

- local authorities and police were struggling to enforce basic standards and reduce crime

- long-standing residents, often in small enclaves, were fighting to hold conditions as properties in the streets around emptied.

Schools

A shrinking population, high population turnover and high levels of deprivation all impact on schools. In turn, school performance affects neighbourhood prospects. Tables 33 and 34 show changes in school rolls, spare places and pupil turnover in the local primary and secondary schools serving one of our neighbourhoods. They also show performance compared with the national average.

The state primary and secondary schools have all suffered from falling rolls and surplus places. This reduction matches the falling ward population and falling numbers of children under 16. The proportion of free school meals, a clear measure of poverty, is extraordinarily high; in two schools it is four times the national average. More than double the national proportion of children in the state primaries had special educational needs. Educational attainment was generally far below the national average, though one primary school scored above the national average in science. The gap by GCSE had widened even further. The outcome measures are crude and make no allowance for the educational difficulties teachers face. Nonetheless, children's life chances are constricted by such low educational attainment.

The performance of the Catholic primary and secondary schools is in sharp contrast. While there are falling numbers of Catholic primary pupils, the school recruits from further afield and makes up numbers with non-Catholic applicants. Figure 5 shows the contrasting trend in school rolls. The Catholic schools have far fewer free school meals and less children with special educational needs. Even allowing for this, they perform better than expected at GCSE and in English at primary level – above the national average. The 'value added' is significant. This is a pattern repeated in Catholic schools in poor areas throughout the country and is worthy of closer study (Catholic Education Service, 1997). It relates to the ethos, pastoral role, approach to discipline, parental support and teaching methods. As yet, educational research has not fully explained the difference.

Demolition of housing immediately surrounding two of the primaries as part of a regeneration programme destabilised the population, including the schools. The regeneration programme within the neighbourhood was removing housing, reducing the number of pupils *and* spending a substantial amount on school buildings and education projects in the area. This contradiction upset teachers as they battled against near impossible odds to save their schools.

Pupil turnover and falling rolls reinforce each other, creating funding problems and loss of morale among staff. Schools can become socially unviable unless extraordinary measures are introduced. Figure 6 shows this.

The poor academic performance of schools in poor neighbourhoods does have a strong deterrent effect on potential residents. It also leads to families with high aspirations moving away (Rudlin, 1998; Urban Task Force, 1999b).

The local authority is developing a new approach to schools with falling rolls in this area. The goal is to retain families with strong loyalty to the school, get parents involved, provide a base for adult education and use surplus space for other council services.

Table 33 Summary of primary school characteristics

School name[1]	School type	% change in roll (1982–97)	% surplus places (January 1998)	% pupil turnover (1994/95)	%FSM[2] (1997)	% pupils with SEN[3] (1997)		% of eligible pupils achieving Level 4 or above in Key Stage 2 tests (1997)		
						Total SEN	With statements[4]	English	Maths	Science
Fieldway	County	–37	34	44	90	76	1	45	48	69
Beech Tree	County	–26	38	19	45	46	4	56	34	51
Grove	County	–29	35	29	82	54	1	22	19	22
All Saints	Voluntary aided (Catholic)	+30	0	0	31	18	1	70	53	53
LEA average	–	–	–	–	–	–	–	51	50.9	60.2
National average	–	–	–	–	22.9	18.5	1.4	62.5	61.3	68.1

Source: LEA and Ofsted. (Where there was a discrepancy between the two sources, the figure closest to the information from the heads' interviews was used.)

1 All school names are invented.

2 FSM = pupils in receipt of free school meals.

3 SEN = pupils with special education needs (expressed as a percentage of the September roll)

4 Statement = pupils with statements of special education needs (expressed as a percentage of the September roll).

Table 34 Summary of secondary school characteristics

School name[1]	School type	% change in roll (1982–97)	% surplus places (January 1998)	% pupil turnover (1997/98)	%FSM[2] (1997)	% pupils with SEN[3] (1997)		GCSE performance (1997)	
						Total SEN	With statements[4]	% achieving 5A–C	% achieving 5 A–G
Thamesway	County	-62	185	~10	56.4	21	1.6	8	50
Octavia	Voluntary aided (Catholic)	+4	4	~0	20.6	10	0.4	54	92
Augustus	Voluntary aided (Catholic)	+2	5	–	19.5	6.6	0.9	52	91
LEA average	–	–	–	–	–	–	–	32	75
National average	–	–	–	–	18.2	16.6	2.3	43.3	88.5

Source: LEA and Ofsted. (Where there was a discrepancy between the two sources, the figure closest to the information from the heads' interviews was used.)

1 All school names are invented.
2 FSM = pupils in receipt of free school meals.
3 SEN = pupils with special education needs (expressed as a percentage of the September roll).
4 Statement = pupils with statements of special education needs (expressed as a percentage of the September roll).
5 The discrepancy between the falling roll and proportion of surplus places is accounted for by a series of school mergers.

Figure 5 Numbers on the roll of each of the secondary schools, 1982–97

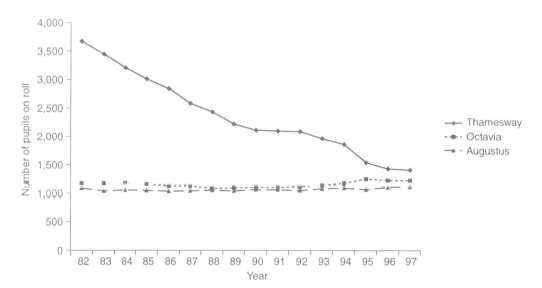

Figure 6 Knock-on effects on school performance

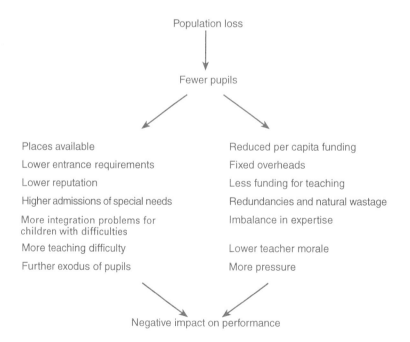

Overall, we found both negative and positive elements in city neighbourhoods.

Table 35 summarises both.

Table 35 Factors influencing city neighbourhoods – based on the Manchester and Newcastle case studies

	Negative elements	Positive elements
Conditions	Multiple inner city decay Sense of emptiness Burnt out property Abandoned facilities, boarded up properties Demolition sites, back alleys, ugly high fences	Near city centre Space – green areas Good housing, some very good Spending on improvements Obvious effort to save area
Services	No overarching plan – or person with power over all services Poor school performance Uncertain commitment of some services to area Departmentalism, centralism, in-fighting Lack of confidence in future Uphill battle Many, frequent setbacks	Some attempts at co-ordination Schools – huge effort Very localised housing service Dedicated local staff Police – strong liaison and anti-crime measures Special initiatives Some impact
Community	Fear, insecurity Loss of confidence Blame attached to youth, newcomers, criminals Some very difficult personalities Some dangerous behaviour and intimidation Strong criticism of police and housing services Growing abandonment	Many stable residents Training and skill building Surprising commitment to saving pockets Strong attachments and networks Energy to keep trying Leading activists Resistance to demolition
Wider issues	Continuing population and job loss General anti-city bias Constant pressures against the poorest inner city neighbourhoods Regeneration spending too focused on physical renewal Too little emphasis on changes in job situation Poor social and economic connections Large-scale unemployment among men High risk/prejudice against inner areas	Strong civic ambition, city pride, loyalty Prestige developments, struggle for resources Reviving city centre – close by Efforts at training and skill building Some new opportunities Easy transport links Job expansion for women and services Fight for inward investment

Part III

The story of four neighbourhoods

This section attempts to convey the live experience of acute decline and the intense efforts to hold on to and rescue inner city neighbourhoods. The story of each area, using the words of local residents and workers, emphasises the gravity of the situation and brings out the potential for rebirth.

7 Bankside

About the area

Bankside is approximately two miles from the city centre, on the riverside. In the past, it was the scene of much industrial activity. However, riverside industries suffered long-term decline and, during the 1970s and 1980s, the remaining industrial base was relocated, encouraged by subsidy. A business park opened nearby in 1990/91 with government incentives. It includes 67 firms, employing 4,800 people. However, the jobs are mostly in the service sector and fewer than 100 local people are employed there. The skills gap is a major obstacle.

Bankside has been losing population over a long period. Demolition has been ongoing since 1992. The landscape is thus constantly changing:

There is no greater portrayal of the transience of an area than demolition. (Social worker)

Bankside's housing is attractive – comprising modernised 1930s' houses with front and rear gardens, and some pre-1919 terraced houses and flats (mostly refurbished by housing associations and private landlords).

How/when it hit trouble

Bankside's current problems have their roots in the industrial restructuring of earlier decades, and the area has long had a reputation for high levels of poverty and serious crime.

By the 1980s, low demand was visible:

Social services have usually been able to get people housed in Bankside – there has always been property available. (Social worker)

The steep increase in empty properties happened between 1989, when there were 40–50 empties, and 1991 when the total had risen to around 350. This coincided with an increase in the amount of crime committed by young men against their own community – burglary, joy-riding and stripping empty houses.

People in work can buy cheaply elsewhere. Those on housing benefit have rented housing to choose from because of surplus housing in the area:

There are bribes to people, almost, to move – furniture packages, redecoration allowances, a newly refurbished property. Although we 'regenerators' think that we're doing this to regenerate the property and make it more attractive, in fact, to some extent, it is just fuelling a revolving door. (Regeneration manager).

Press coverage has added to Bankside's negative image. Pictures of boarded up homes and young children vandalising properties carry headlines such as 'Little Beirut'.

One new-build housing association development is empty, some of the houses never having been let since they were built. Part of it is now due to be demolished. Another housing association owns 44 refurbished, pepper-potted street properties. Nineteen were empty at May 1998. High quality council houses have no demand:

The allocations policy is basically: 'Do you want a house?' (Senior council officer)

Not all parts of Bankside have been hit equally severely. There are pockets of stability which are a different world from the half-empty streets just minutes away. Even within the emptying streets, committed long-standing residents surrounded by boarded up homes, continue to attempt to create their own stability, with courage, tenacity, solidarity and pride.

Extended family networks on particular estates can be the main factor in their stability:

I love it – I feel very settled here. In Lower Bankside, everyone is part of an extended family, and that's the only reason we stay there. (Resident)

Equally, these networks can mean that, once one household decides to go, several move out at once because of their family ties and their desire to move together.

Bankside is fragile, and vulnerable to rapid change. Often, residents and community workers identify one factor as the immediate trigger:

The council allocated a property to a vulnerable man who attracted a lot of other young men to congregate there. The neighbours on each side left, and, over six months, the street steadily emptied. Now, one side of the road is going to be demolished. (Tenant support worker)

Since the fieldwork was completed, the other side of this road is now also being demolished.

Inputs/impacts

Bankside's problems have long been recognised by central and local government. Local politicians and residents' groups have successfully fought for resources. The Urban Programme of the late 1970s, and more recent regeneration efforts such as Safer Cities, Estate Action and City Challenge, have injected many millions of pounds into the area. These projects have slowed the decay. But impacts often lasted only as long as the programmes:

Five-year projects are no use at all. An area like this needs help in a sustained way. The people here want to help themselves, but they need help to do it. (Primary school head)

Residents

Fed up with the stigma, the desolation of living in a half-empty street, the harassment and vandalism, and tempted by housing on offer elsewhere, many residents have left:

A relatively minor incident can prompt people to take flight. (Local researcher)

A primary school head started to keep a record of the reasons for people moving but stopped doing this when she discovered that most left because of harassment of some kind; serious, targeted harassment resulting from someone informing to the police, or more general threatening behaviour.

A survey of residents in one emptying street revealed that 50 per cent of the residents found it 'terrible/frightening' to live in a street with so many empty properties, causing worry and depression. The main factors causing people to leave were crime and fear of crime, intimidation by gangs of young people, harassment and anti-social behaviour by other tenants (Community Group report, 1996):

Putting on a porch and landscaping the garden doesn't really do anything – it's all very cosmetic. People will drive through the area now and think 'oh, it's not that bad, these houses look really nice'. But it's to do with people. Somehow we've got to get hold of these families that are bullying the neighbourhood and shift them … somewhere. (Primary school head)

Other residents are happy to live in the only place that they have ever known as home, amongst their family and friends:

Where would I go anyway? I'm staying where I'm used to. (Resident)

Some residents have continued to fight in an organised way to achieve the improvements that they want. An estate housing management committee was formed in 1995 and extended last year to cover the whole neighbourhood. The committee meets regularly with the local council housing manager, monitors the housing service and has an input into policy. The tenants' groups are also supporting newcomers to Bankside. Security is their number one priority. Under the combined efforts of residents and local housing staff, many new approaches have been tried:

- show houses

- estate walkabouts

- patch reports by estate officers

- local display boards showing property available for letting

- a drop-in session for new tenants with local staff

- dedicated estate labourers

- rapid-response void clear-out

- tenants' reporting channels.

In spite of these efforts, failures still arise.

Housing management

The council has a full-time local housing office in Bankside. Staff are attempting to develop closer working with residents and are 'extremely committed to this difficult area'. Constructive work with the police is ongoing:

We are turning streets around by getting rid of problematic families, achieving a good standard of repairs, tidying up the voids, and concentrating our efforts. (Council officer)

However, it remains very hard to attract people into Bankside:

People don't want to come to Bankside because they think it's rough. (Council officer)

Schools

Three of the four primaries in the area have suffered from falling rolls since 1988. Their pupil populations are extremely deprived.

Families often show attachment to the schools, moving away but continuing to send their children to the school until the journey involved becomes too much to manage.

The main secondary school serving the area failed its Ofsted inspection in 1995/96. This exacerbated its falling roll and added to the negative reputation of the area. Although the school came out of special measures in December 1997 and the roll has now stabilised, the deprivation of the pupil population has an enormous impact:

We have all sorts of social problems to deal with: children who are malnourished, who are abused, who can see no value in education because they're the fourth generation of unemployed people, and they live on an estate with high levels of crime, fluid movement of population, poverty … (Secondary school head)

Police

The relationship between the police and the community has improved in recent years:

> In the late 1980s, the police had a very negative view of Bankside and its residents – they referred to it as 'the swamp'. The police response has definitely improved since then, and police cars can now be seen in the area every day. (Community development worker)

A range of policing initiatives has been implemented, including a witness support scheme, joint working with housing, schools and residents, and an arson task force (run jointly with the fire brigade).

Unreported crime is a cause for concern, though:

> Witness intimidation and fear of reprisals is a major issue. (Senior police officer)

There are a small number of key troublemakers:

> There are 20 main persistent juvenile offenders in the area command. If we got rid of them, we could dramatically reduce crime. (Police officer)

Current options

Thirty-seven per cent of the council's 1991 stock has been demolished but this has not got rid of the empty properties. If demolition continues to be the main response to streets that are emptying, then Bankside will be incrementally razed to the ground.

As long as people view Bankside as an impoverished, crime-ridden area, and as long as they can gain access to attractive housing elsewhere, its downward spiral will continue. So far, the entrenched negative image, local media attention and general low demand have overpowered attempts to market the area.

The wider social and economic problems need to be given serious attention:

> If as much investment as went into improvements to the housing stock and housing management service had gone into local training, advice and resources to help people into decent paid jobs, it is possible that the decline would have been halted by now. (Community development worker)

Bankside has huge potential. Its housing is not only adequate, it is excellent. Proximity to the city centre and to major road networks is in its favour. Just a few miles away are thriving areas. Security and reputation– neighbourhood quality as well as housing quality – are clearly crucial:

> The city has plans to extend onto the greenbelt because people do like to move out. But we have a site here that if it were ten miles further along the river would be worth millions. It's south facing, it's sunny, and the views are stunning. There's no capital being made of the location. (Primary school head)

However, there is talk at city level of developers being drawn by the regeneration potential of this neighbourhood.

8 City-Edge

About the area

The rows of late nineteenth-century terraces built in City-Edge for people working in nearby industries were largely cleared during the 1960s and 1970s. Council houses, maisonettes and deck access flats replaced them. Some pockets of better quality terraced housing escaped clearance. Eleven of these streets, in a grid-iron pattern, make up Lower City-Edge, which was rejuvenated temporarily when it was declared a Housing Action Area in the 1970s. The deck access flats were notorious from the day they were built, and survived for only 15 years before being demolished and replaced by new council houses in the 1990s. Private companies have also built homes within the last nine years and housing associations were completing new houses as recently as 1995. Even so, there remain large patches of open, grassed-over demolition sites.

Parts of City-Edge are nearly 50 per cent empty. Some homes are physically inadequate – with structural problems or unpopular design features. However, there are traditionally designed, modern, well built houses, with front and back gardens, for which there is zero demand. Much of the owner occupied housing has either transferred to the private rented sector or been abandoned completely. The council has estimated that two-thirds of houses in a private development of 80 homes are now rented rather than owner occupied. Fifty-eight of the 138 privately owned homes in Lower City-Edge were empty at October 1998.

City-Edge has always been a poor area, but people used to have a reason for living there – they had work nearby. By the late 1980s, however, most of the traditional engineering, textiles and steel jobs had been lost:

You can keep on patching up the housing, but, unless you actually have a reason for people wanting to be there, then you've lost it.
(Local councillor)

It's been a transit zone for a long time – with all the clearance, refurbishment and new building. Some people have moved from one bit of housing to the next.
(Community development worker)

How/when it hit trouble

In the second half of the 1980s, people recognised the loss of demand:

We had a very stable community on our estate until 1986, when the local Tenants' Association succeeded in getting the properties modernised. All 53 residents were decanted in order for the works to take place, but only five households chose to move back in afterwards. There was no general hatred of the properties, it was just that their circumstances had changed. We had these new, modernised properties but people didn't want to move into them. (Local councillor)

In other parts of City-Edge, acute low demand has appeared within the last six years. The immediate causes were crime, vandalism and serious anti-social behaviour:

Everyone leaves this area for the same reason: they fear for their safety.
(Housing association officer)

I want to move now. Although I've never been mithered by the gangs and I've never been robbed, I'm frightened. (Resident)

In the absence of demand, landlords felt that they had no option but to let to whoever applied. A concentration of large families with problems in one estate was responsible for years of serious anti-social behaviour, which in the end caused even the most determined of long-standing residents to leave. The council followed eviction procedures but these were lengthy – it took two years to secure the eviction of the most troublesome family and, although they now live in another part of the city, they still harass those who gave evidence against them. An injunction was obtained; the father of this family recently served a 28-day prison sentence for ten breaches of it.

Blocks of one-bed flats in the area had traditionally been let to the elderly. As elderly tenants died (and in the absence of elderly applicants) the council let the flats to young single people. The combination of young and old in an unsupervised, insecure environment did not work. The young tenants appeared out of control and the elderly were terrified.

> People say if you put a rotten apple in the middle, it changes and becomes good. But that doesn't work. It just clears the building. And it happens very rapidly. When I was new in the job, I moved a young man into a block of six flats that had a stable, elderly community who'd lived there for years. Within five to six weeks, five of the flats were empty. He was abusive. He tried to rob them. He had all his mates there too. (Council housing officer)

The housing associations continued to build, but often let their new accommodation to people who were already resident in the area. As one council housing officer commented:

> Forty-four housing association properties were completed nearby in 1995. I must have had between 20 and 25 tenants, out of my patch of about 300, move into those properties.

Impacts/inputs

Residents

Abandonment problems aren't uniform throughout City-Edge. On at least three of the six council estates, there remains a stable core of residents who have lived in their houses since the day they were built. These estates have strong and well established tenants' associations or Homewatch schemes – formed in the mid-1990s in response to a deteriorating living environment and community disintegration. On two estates, there is not a single empty house.

Some residents have had enough. They've tried to change things but the violence that they have faced, and their frustration at the delay in public intervention, has finally prompted them to try to move away:

> If I thought, for one minute, I could make a difference, I would stay. (Resident)

People have seen their life's investment become virtually worthless:

> One bloke has lived there for 50 years. He raised his kids in the property and it was a struggle for him to pay off the mortgage. So he comes to retire, with this property behind him. He's paid off the mortgage – but it isn't worth a carrot to him. And such a proud person who felt that when he passed away he could pass that house to his kids. Well, his kids don't want it. (Local councillor)

Relationships on the ground can be vital to maintaining the confidence of residents. New approaches can help:

The improvement in allocations management by the council means that existing tenants have more confidence. They are no longer 'panic-stricken' about who will move in next door because they know that it will be someone decent. Before, people were so terrified about who would move in, that they would be looking to move away just in case. (Resident)

The system of the TA [Tenants' Association] recommending people worked well on our estate. Through this practice, we increased the stability of the estate and the sense of community. There are four generations of one family living on the estate and three generations of another. We want to encourage this. That's what builds up the community we want. (Resident)

Housing service

The high level of empty homes obviously reduces the housing department's income. The high turnover and need to secure empty properties increases costs. There are intangible costs, such as the effect on staff morale. Housing officers are faced daily with the misery of people being harassed and intimidated. Pressure to fill empties conflicts with the dire consequences of an insensitive letting:

As soon as people moved on to this estate they were being robbed of everything they'd got. You feel responsible – I put them there and this happened to them. It just completely blows your mind. (Housing officer)

The housing service is up-front about its

failures, some of which frustrate residents terribly:

We've been terrible in our management of the area. What's needed is all the basics – local patch officers getting out and about, spotting things early, being proactive. But it's easier said than done in an area like this. It all becomes too much for people and they get overwhelmed by it. (Council officer)

Housing staff should visit the people in the houses more – and see what's going on. They only see you if there's a problem. They should just pop round and sort things out early on. (Resident)

Even the most dedicated and proactive housing team cannot deliver a quality service on its own. The housing department set up a neighbourhood strategies working party in September 1997, involving social services, the police, community groups, schools and others. This group has worked together on child supervision:

Children from target families feel that their behaviour is being closely monitored by various agencies … children were complaining of being watched from all sides at school, at home and when they were playing in the local area. (Council report, 1998)

Departments have traditionally worked in isolation and some services, by their very nature, come with different perspectives. The 'area overview' role of housing and the 'individual advocacy' role of social services can conflict when, for example, the eviction of families with problems is considered. Without special follow-through, an eviction to solve a housing problem can create a costly social casualty. The new approach is requiring a great deal of effort to implement in practice, both between and within departments.

Schools

School numbers have fallen and some schools fear closure. High turnover also affects them. For example, in just a few months, one of the primary schools lost 22 children but gained 18 others.

The crime in the area can also affect school buildings and grounds. In May 1998, one of the primaries had 16 burnt out cars on its premises within just three days (Council report, 1998).

Police

The police service is perceived very differently in different parts of City-Edge. Members of one of the Homewatch schemes spoke highly of the local community police officer and of the close working relationship that had been established. Police and housing have also worked together effectively, although both see gaps. But, in certain parts of the area, police officers are not visible on the ground:

I'm not anti-police, but the police manpower for these areas is just a joke. (Estate agent)

Some residents feel let down by the police:

One night there were about 60 people gathered on the corner of our street with ghetto blasters. I rang the police at 2.00 a.m., and they said to me 'What do you want us to do about it?' (Resident)

Shopping

The shopping centre has declined steadily over the past ten years:

You can almost test the temperature of the community by how many shops there are, how many disappear, what sorts of goods are being sold. We've seen a gradual run-down of the shopping centre. The bank moved out in 1989/90. There is still a post office, but it's not thriving. There are at least half a dozen derelict shops, whereas, in the early 1970s, they were all open. (Senior manager, social services)

Current options

A neighbourhood renewal assessment advised clearance of Lower City-Edge. The statutory process is not yet complete and there have been objections, but many owner occupiers are pleased, especially given the degree of dilapidation that now exists:

Clearance is the only way forward. I just want to get out quick. (Resident)

Residents breathed a huge sigh of relief when they heard that the result of the neighbourhood renewal assessment was to recommend clearance. (Council officer)

The main housing association in Lower City-Edge has decided that there is no alternative but to demolish homes completed only eight years ago, but surrounded by empty terraced houses. Already selective demolition of one-bed flats has helped appearances. Demolition of some of the houses has proved less successful. The houses adjoining one demolition site are now boarded up. The problem of too few people and too many houses remains, with the associated uncertainty, lettings dilemmas and extreme polarisation that are so damaging to City-Edge, already at the bottom of the city's housing market.

A large leisure development is being built on the edge of the area, and this may bring jobs, an extension of the metro and new life for the neighbourhood. The city is proposing City-Edge for a major regeneration initiative. Great expectations surround the new approach. This initiative signals light at the end of the tunnel. Investment will need to be linked to sustained basic inputs – cleaning, repairs, tenant involvement, support for new tenants, careful lettings and co-ordination across services.

9 Riverview

About the area

Riverview lies less than two miles from the city centre; 30 minutes' walk along the river. This area has a long history of industrial activity, including coal mining, iron and chemical works, shipbuilding and related engineering industries. During the 1980s, key employers scaled down their workforces and eventually closed altogether. With the support of the local authority and the Urban Development Corporation, a technology park was created. However:

> *The few jobs that are around now are not suitable for the unskilled workers from Riverview. (Regeneration manager)*

Council housing dominates the area. Inter-war estates of two- and three-bed terraced and semi-detached houses with front and rear gardens were modernised from the 1970s, providing attractive, good quality houses. Post-war developments included houses, maisonettes, multi-storey and 'scissor blocks'. Some were demolished recently because of their unpopular design and low demand.

> *Why did they insist on building maisonette flats? – families on families. (Resident)*

Housing associations own a small amount of refurbished and new-build property.

How/when it hit trouble

Riverview is divided into several distinct parts. Lower Riverview has always been stigmatised, because of its location near the now defunct heavy industry:

> *When I was young, Lower Riverview was the 'lowest of the low'. I only went down there for Chapel and Sunday School. There was nothing else to go down for. It was a bad place. (Resident)*

However, people used to have a reason for living in Riverview; they had employment nearby:

> *The relationship between houses, the community and employment in the area was extremely important. People would walk or cycle to work and the community was able to see what they were building – it created an enormous sense of pride. (Regeneration manager)*

Once these links to local employment no longer existed, the community began to fragment:

> *There has been an increasing number of single parents, short-lived relationships and a shifting population which has a destabilising effect on estates. There are a large number of men wandering around different relationships leaving a lot of unsettled and damaged people behind them. (Senior council officer)*

People became demoralised. Those who did find employment tended to move out to become owner occupiers in nearby areas. The loss of local employment occurred at a time when it was becoming much easier to enter owner occupation:

> *It is not very expensive to enter owner occupation: the cost per month is less than a council rent if you're working. (Former resident)*

The least popular housing, and those areas that were already stigmatised, began to experience demand problems. By January 1998, every fifth house in Lower Riverview was empty:

People from outside won't even come to view the properties here because of its reputation. (Resident)

Not enough people want to come and live in Lower Riverview – it's out of the way, at the bottom of the bank and it is overlooking an area where once there used to be local employment but is no longer. It is at the bottom of the pecking order of local authority housing. (Regeneration manager)

Historical allocations policies that graded people and areas contributed to that place in the pecking order:

A ghetto was manufactured. In the 1970s, the allocation process graded people A, B, C, D, or Z. Certain estates started getting a greater proportion of Z-graded people. The area manager used to use it as a threat … and tell people that, if they didn't pay their rent, they'd be rehoused in Lower Riverview. (Council officer)

The slack in the system was further increased by the development of 70 housing association homes in 1996:

This site became available for letting right at a time when demand was plummeting. It has had a disastrous impact on Lower Riverview. (Council officer)

However, this development was initiated by local residents and built on land previously occupied by derelict factories which was an eyesore. It illustrates conflicting political, financial, local and organisational interests:

The development of this estate originated from meetings of parents at the primary school and the Development Corporation encouraged it. We knew it would create voids in the local authority stock, but the council had no choice. They couldn't have sabotaged a people-led enterprise and couldn't have said 'no' because of the powers of the Development Corporation. In any case, the council wanted people to think for themselves and local members supported it. Obviously, housing officers were worried … (Local councillor)

More recently the demand problems have spread northwards, affecting the parts of Riverview that had been regarded as more stable and less stigmatised. There are few empty houses, but turnover is high. Blocks of flats are continually being demolished.

The local authority sector has borne the brunt of falling demand over the past ten years. However, older terraced private stock on the main road has suffered a rapid decline. By January 1998, 31 units were vacant out of a total of 99:

Central Road went downhill very rapidly, just in the last 18 months. There was a domino effect – people started leaving in their droves. (Community development officer)

The housing on this road had been nearly all owner occupied but, in a very short space of time, houses and flats were transferred to the private rented sector. As elderly owner occupiers died, private landlords bought up their houses:

There is evidence that social unrest has been engineered by people who want to purchase housing on Central Road at knockdown rates.

Owners are forced to sell and the new landlords then let to housing benefit claimants.
(Senior police officer)

This has shocked local people:

Central Road used to be posh. Those were lovely flats. It breaks your heart. I wouldn't live in them rent-free now, but they used to be elite.
(Resident)

Inputs/impacts

Residents

Riverview retains a number of tightly knit communities. Family networks provide a reason for people remaining in the area even though work has gone. However, it can be off-putting to 'outsiders':

The negative side of the sense of community that exists is that it can be very parochial. Anyone born more than half a mile away is an alien. Anyone who's different in any way is not made to feel welcome at all. (Council officer)

There are two tenants' groups and a small core of committed activists. One group succeeded in saving a former social services day centre from being demolished. With support from the council, and from the Single Regeneration Budget, it has since been converted into a community centre with an attached community development worker. A range of groups and council services now uses it.

Residents were also instrumental in establishing a community-run security project in Lower Riverview, based in one of the tower blocks. It was set up in 1993 and comprises CCTV, a 24-hour door guard, and a security patrol. Action is co-ordinated with the housing service and the police. The project employs local people:

Since the security project commenced, reported crime has fallen significantly. We have driven the bad people away. When the security project first started, there were more than 20 voids out of the 85 flats in the tower. This has been reduced to seven. (Security project manager)

The local church has played an important role in supporting these community initiatives. However:

The residents' association needs to take Lower Riverview forward, but it has dwindled over the past few years. It feels as though people don't care. (Resident)

As well as a stable core, there is a transient population:

People move up the bank as quickly as they can – so there's a constant change of people. (Youth officer)

There are a small number of families who have a disproportionately negative impact on the area:

One notorious family was responsible for five years of harassment, crime and burglaries. They established a little kingdom down there – it was completely wild. (Council officer)

There is a feeling that there has been a more general shift in attitudes and behaviour:

The housing has got better, but the neighbours have got worse. Before it used to be: 'Don't touch that, it's the council'. Now it's: 'Do wreck it because it's the council'. (Resident)

The serious unemployment which exists causes a black economy, because people just can't manage on benefits. If they declared this income, they would lose everything because of the poverty trap. But the realisation by youngsters that their fathers have got to get by through 'fiddling' is not helpful. (Local councillor)

Housing

The council is faced with a difficult dilemma. It needs to fill the properties, and neither local nor citywide adverts have had much success:

People with mental health problems have been foisted on housing and they've housed them because they're under pressure to make allocations with demand falling. (Regeneration manager)

People are aware that if you give up your council home today and your next place doesn't work out, you can be offered somewhere else again very quickly. This has the effect of devaluing council housing. It's a trap that we're in. We're not going to turn people away. (Senior council officer)

The housing department should vet new tenants. If they've been thrown out from other parts of the city, why should we have them? (Resident)

However, the housing service has taken this on board with its deferral policy for people responsible for anti-social behaviour. And it has been a force for good – maintaining a presence on the ground, addressing historical service problems, working closely with the security project and the police, and continually attempting to halt the spread of voids. The back-up it needs from other council services is often lacking:

Housing is left out there as the last front-line service, underpinning housing demand and addressing the lack of social cohesion. (Renewal manager)

It is not easy:

The situation is now beyond our control – despite trying every trick in the book to reduce voids, including advertising. (Council officer)

Police

The police work closely with the housing service and the security project. They also exchange information with probation, the schools and social services, and are actively involved with the SRB programme. Crime has been reduced through the proactive targeting of persistent offenders.

There is serious organised crime and people's perceptions of crime are hard to change:

Although the crime rate has fallen, there is a problem of perception. The old and the vulnerable have retreated. (Community co-ordinator)

In Lower Riverview, the problems and tensions that used to exist are no longer. But the name is still a powerful negative. (Senior police officer)

Part of the police strategy is to talk positively about the area. Youth initiatives include regular visits to schools by a 'youth issues officer', police forums for 14–16 year olds and a volunteer cadet force.

Some residents argue that the police are still not visible enough:

We would like to see more police walking the beat. (Residents)

Schools

All schools serve a very deprived population:

The long-term and growing unemployment has undermined the social fabric of the area. Many students have reading ages over two years below their actual ages.
(Ofsted report of secondary school, 1996)

In a situation of high unemployment, it can be hard to demonstrate the benefits of education:

As a careers teacher, I could take pupils to the shipyards and they could apply for (and mostly get) apprenticeships followed by jobs for life. Tremendous efforts are being made to encourage children to stay on at school – but it's very hard if they can't see any opportunity at the end of it all.
(Secondary school head)

One primary school, in partnership with parents, pupils, governors and outside agencies, developed play facilities, a community wing (in which a range of courses are held), crèche facilities and a community library. It runs a Breakfast Club, sponsored by local businesses. Sixty to 70 children attend this every day:

The school has to be more than a school in an area like this. (Primary school head)

Departmental boundaries can be frustrating:

With a community that's dying, where there's no hope, you need a joint long-term approach, not a situation where everyone is working in little boxes. I've spent ten years fighting these little boxes to get the school where it is today.
(Primary school head)

The school's roll increased by 47 per cent between 1982 and 1997. Other primaries in the area haven't fared so well, two having suffered from falling rolls for decades.

Current options

Selective demolition of some council blocks has had a positive impact on the private housing overlooking them. The council will carry out improvements to the remaining maisonette blocks. In Lower Riverview, there may be further selective demolition to remove the blight of empty homes. However, there is a danger that the 'front line of the voids' will creep further up the bank.

A regeneration programme is under way. The focus is on people, services, jobs and support, as well as on buildings. There will be environmental improvements rather than redevelopment. Additional social housing is not wanted here:

There is something fundamentally wrong with the perception of council housing. It needs rebranding. (Renewal manager)

Most of Riverview is not yet locked into abandonment. But Riverview is hovering on the brink and, according to the senior manager, there is no waiting list at all for the area. If the existing community can be persuaded to stay, then Riverview can survive for the time being. But the population is ageing and times have changed. The old way of life depended on local, manual employment. New employment opportunities will be vital to the social cohesion of the area and to give people a reason to live in Riverview. Whilst the drain from city estates into owner occupation continues, Riverview's future hangs in the balance.

10 Valleyside

About the area

Although Valleyside is an inner city area, it contains many open spaces and parks. Parts of it have almost a 'village feel'. It has good shopping facilities, including a large Asda.

Valleyside has always been a working class area. Most major employers left the area approximately ten years ago:

> *Without employment, the area is not sustainable. Unless you get these people back into work, you're wasting your time.* (Private sector officer)

Nearly 60 per cent of Valleyside's housing is terraced. The pre-1919 houses are small, opening directly on to the pavement, with shared alleys at the rear. There are also eight local authority estates, built in the 1960s and 1970s. One has been significantly redeveloped. Others suffer from poor design, a high proportion of flats and maisonettes, disrepair, unsupervised open areas and unkempt environments. Housing associations have been involved in refurbishment of pre-1919 housing and have also built anew during the 1990s.

How/when it hit trouble

A demand problem only became visible across Valleyside in the last three years, although some individual estates have had high turnover since much earlier.

Allocations policies during the 1980s and early 1990s emphasised housing and social need to the exclusion of other applicants. The result was a high concentration of people who were unable to cope on particular estates. Meanwhile, waiting lists dried up. Slack in the system meant that people who wanted to leave could do so:

> *It took time for us to recognise the extent of the change that was happening and to introduce policies to counteract the detrimental effect of this.* (Senior council officer)

> *Everyone who wanted to be let in to this estate was let in.* (Council officer)

All tenures are now affected by low demand. In nearby private terraces, approximately 20 per cent of properties are empty; up from 5 per cent just two years ago. This overall figure masks the fact that there are stable, fully occupied streets as well as streets which are virtually deserted.

A housing association development completed four years ago created more choice and had the knock-on effect of further reducing demand for the unpopular council stock:

> *Between 30 per cent and 40 per cent of the tenants came out of our council dwellings in adjacent estates ... the stock is better designed and better laid-out.* (Regeneration manager)

Poor management in the private sector has added to problems:

> *Low demand is to do with the way that landlords haven't been managing their properties, and their lettings policy – or lack of one.* (Resident)

As the population of the terraces grows older, and the younger generation is increasingly uninterested in buying such housing, the proportion of private renting will continue to increase. Areas have changed rapidly if elderly residents have died at around the same time:

> *In our street we've got quite a high percentage of older residents. They get intimidated. If you get two or three problem families, the houses start to*

deteriorate, the elderly move on and other people come in of a similar character. It's like a cycle. If one house gets empty and gets vandalised, very shortly you'll find another one goes the same way. Over a short period of time, a quarter or even a third of a street can die like that, quite quickly. (Resident)

Inputs/impacts

Housing/regeneration

One estate has been completely renewed including attractive new housing and renovated tower blocks. The local authority confirms it has healthy demand though it needs sustained input from staff and residents. According to the local housing officer, it is drawing tenants from other estates. A bid to regenerate a neighbouring estate failed.

Private companies are building homes for sale, with subsidy from English Partnerships. This is being done as an 'act of faith' – in the belief that demand will be generated by supplying the right quality housing. Of the 169 sales completed or reserved in the regeneration area so far, 60 per cent have been to existing city residents (possibly stopping people exiting the city). Forty per cent of sales are to incomers, who are being attracted to live in the city. So far, the homes are at the cheaper end of the market and almost 60 per cent of sales have been to purchasers earning no more than £15,000 per annum (Council report, September 1998). One company plans to build 250 homes in Valleyside.

Work is ongoing to attract businesses into the area, build up the local skills base and link local residents with employment opportunities. Regenerators are joining with youth workers to include young people in this.

Renewal of pre-1919 terraces is focused on those parts of the area with the strongest resident interest. Until recently, housing associations were using social housing grant to acquire and renew properties. Gradual renewal and selective clearance will continue.

The local authority has also focused on improving conditions through intensive management, setting clear standards of behaviour and enforcing those standards. A furnished tenancy scheme has reduced empty flats in multi-storey blocks. The council has actively sought to redress past failures. It has forged strong links with the police, as have housing associations. However, the estate suffering the worst demand problems in the area has continued to deteriorate:

We've been trying to manage our way through the problems on this estate, because we weren't able to put in the capital investment that we did elsewhere. We've got very intensive management there: allocations procedures with pre-offer checks. We've got an inter-agency task force, and we've shifted the crime and nuisance off the estate. But we have not made one jot of impact on demand. (Regeneration manager)

It's not working. (Council officer)

The level of empty properties is a continual drain on the housing service:

Empty properties drag the estate down and waste a lot of time, energy and resources. A lot of money has been wasted keeping empties secure. (Council officer)

Housing staff were surprised when they canvassed opinion about demolition on this estate which was 35 per cent empty at March 1998. Contrary to expectations, they found that a majority wanted to stay. This was despite being surrounded by empty houses; a few so badly vandalised and decayed that entire sections of wall are missing, revealing the interior of rooms.

Residents

There are strong communities in Valleyside:

Valleyside has got some very stable communities that function and exercise social control. (Senior council officer)

There is a warmth in Valleyside – there is this community feeling. (Head teacher)

Residents have been instrumental in the changed fortunes of the renewed estate. The residents' association there was established in 1985:

When you live in a community, you don't notice what's happening about you. You walk over the rubbish, you pass the empty houses, you get used to your environment. For me, the initial point was when I was going to work one day and a used nappy came flying out of a flat and landed at my feet. I stood there thinking; 'God, this is what we've come to'. That was the starting point. I thought; 'Something's got to be done'. (Leading resident activist)

There is also an unstable population:

We've seen an increase in the transient population. (Resident)

Some residents feel disaffected:

There's a lack of hope for some people … and that pervades the area. (Resident)

There is a limit to how much people will tolerate, especially when there is plenty of alternative housing on offer:

People do want to stay in the area, but they don't have to live around empty properties – they don't have to live next door to the local drug dealer – they can just get up and move somewhere else. (Housing association officer)

Schools

Some schools face closure because of surplus places, including a secondary which was recently refurbished at a cost of £1.2 million. The roll of one of the primaries fell from 380 to 207 between 1993 and 1998:

One of the biggest things we're battling against is pupil numbers. (School governor)

By the end of Key Stage 2 (aged ten–11), out of a class of 25, only half have been here from the beginning. (Primary school head)

One of the primaries has had a drive to improve attendance and to reach out into the community. The head is keen to get parents involved in education themselves, in the belief that they will then attach greater importance to their children's attendance and progress:

So many of our parents condone absence from school. If parents have been through the system and they've not come out with this feeling of the importance of reading and learning having a value of its own, how can they impart that to their children? So we've got a breakfast club, we've resurrected the parent-toddler group and we've opened up the school for adult education classes. (Primary school head)

Initially, there was a significant

improvement in attendance and punctuality but, as the year has gone on, this has dropped off. However, the initiatives have been successful in involving more parents and a PTA has been set up.

Police

The police service has adopted a joint-working approach, with the housing service, the local schools and social services. This has increased the co-operation of the community and other services:

There was a period of very poor relations between the town hall and the police, which started in the early 1980s. If I got some information about someone dealing drugs in a local authority property and I wanted to know who lived there, I'd be told that they don't co-operate with the police. Now, housing actually bring information to us. (Senior police officer)

The crime rate has gone down, mine is one of the quieter beats. (Police officer)

There is still a perception of high crime:

Some people think they are living in the depths of hell. (Council officer)

Some intimidation does not involve anyone actually committing a 'crime':

The younger generation – kids running round the streets, causing nuisance –has the biggest effect on people ... together with drugs.
(Senior police officer)

The empty properties can be a target for children to vandalise:

In some ways, it's like a playground for kids. Once they get a door off, it's an adventure.
(Police officer)

Current options

There is a great deal of regeneration activity in Valleyside. One estate has been completely remodelled, private housing is being selectively cleared and improved, and, most significantly, private developers are building housing for sale (albeit at the lower end of the market and with subsidy). People from outside the city, as well as existing residents, are being attracted into this stock. The crucial test will be whether this new owner occupation is sustained.

There are 125 acres of development land in the regeneration area. It is close to the city centre and the metro will be extended to the area in the next three years. There are, therefore, significant opportunities for job creation and further housing developments for higher income households. There is political support for this strategy. Valleyside has a better chance than other inner city areas of being 'saved', repopulated and 'depolarised':

If you're pessimistic about Valleyside, you're pessimistic about every single inner city area in the country. The problems will be solved. But it is not going to happen overnight.
(Senior council officer)

Alongside the large-scale, dramatic building projects, there needs to be continued intensive support to the existing communities in both the social and private housing:

We need good publicity for the area and for the school. We need private landlords to market their property – with a very strict lettings policy. We want people who are going to be committed to the area and committed to maintaining the property. (Resident)

Ultimately, hope hinges on economic regeneration of the area and the city – giving people a reason to live in Valleyside, and to invest in the area both economically and socially.

Part IV
The causes and consequences of decline

11 The long roots of the problem – history not news

In this part of the report, we try to set the population and job losses in Manchester and Newcastle in the wider context of urban change and decline. We link the local fortunes of the four neighbourhoods to inner city clearance and estate building. We then look at government and local regeneration attempts within a globalising economy that treats cities like Manchester and Newcastle particularly harshly.

In abbreviating and simplifying history, we refer the reader to detailed sources.

Pre-World War I

The roots of abandonment are tangled. The depopulation of cities in Britain has been virtually continuous since before the First World War (Thompson, 1990). Core areas started to depopulate even before the end of the nineteenth century when railways made commuting possible and Britain lost its industrial mastery of the world (Briggs, 1983). By 1900, 80 per cent of the population was urbanised and the pressures to decongest cities were intense. The vast majority of working people in England were living in single family terraced houses, mostly solidly built, opening on to paved streets, with piped water. This housing form was a sign of our relative affluence compared with our continental and Scottish counterparts who were often living in high density tenements (Burnett, 1978). But the density was huge compared with today – 40 dwellings to the acre, six people to a household, at least 240 people to an acre, but rising to 400 in poor city neighbourhoods.

Often, strong support networks developed in these areas, some based on kinship, some on mutual aid principles amongst groups of workers (Thompson, 1990).

Inter-war years

'Coronation Street' neighbourhoods went into rapid decline between the wars when a vast stock of new suburban housing was built, much of it for working people (Burnett, 1978; Holmans, 1987).

Rents were tightly controlled except when re-let to new tenants and nineteenth-century inner city housing decayed rapidly (Holland, 1965). The total supply of homes jumped from seven million to 11 million in 20 short years, much of the increase going to first time, working class owner occupation, as well as to council housing. Suburbs spread and councils created 'peripheral estates' for the first time (Daunton, 1987). People began to be pushed out of the old terraces by slum clearance declarations that in the 1930s rose to one-and-a-half million although only a quarter of a million were actually cleared before the war (Holmans, 1987). Households shrank to an average of three people as the number of homes and households multiplied. This rapid process of deconcentration was abruptly halted by World War Two.

Post-World War II

An ambitious plan to build new estates, new towns and new neighbourhoods was born of war-time solidarity. In order to deliver Utopian estate plans, it was essential to clear two million surviving nineteenth-century slums. These colossal and costly projects blighted every major inner city in Britain from the early 1950s right up to 1980 (Burns, 1963; Power, 1987). Between 1931 and 1978, city populations plummeted, in spite of continuous rebuilding. Aneurin Bevan's dream of recreating English and Welsh villages was corrupted into large monolithic, single tenure, single class estates (Foot, 1973; DoE 1977; Power, 1987). The blight on inner city neighbourhoods, often lasting 30 years or more, destroyed not only many established communities, but also many jobs and services (Young and Wilmott, 1957; Maclennan, 1997; DoE, 1977). There was in fact a deep contradiction between the gains of the mass housing programme in dwellings and amenities, and the upheavals it caused (Dunleavy, 1981).

Urban depopulation

City depopulation was caused by stronger forces than clearance and mass construction of council estates, important as these were. Britain's slow economic decline relative to New World and German expansion from around 1870 turned world famous industrial nerve-centres into over-sized ghosts of history (Briggs, 1983). Rent controls encouraged private landlords to let inner city property fall into disrepair, leading to withdrawal. The 70-year slow boom in owner occupation continuously sucked working and middle class families out of cities into suburban and smaller settlements (Saunders, 1990); but also led to gentrification of older, inner city housing. According to F.H.L. Thompson, dominant owner occupation at the expense of private renting confirmed Britain as a less

mobile society with more class rigidity than other wealthy societies (Thompson, 1990).

The outward movement of jobs and people was actively encouraged from 1930 to 1975 with the aim of reducing overcrowding, cleaning up cities and planning orderly settlements. Some industry in cities like Newcastle was forced out. This reinforced industrial decline and economic restructuring. Thousands of monofunctional estates, stripped of noisy, dirty workshops and cheap corner shops, were built as dormitories for the families of mainly male workers (Community Development Project, 1976).

Severed networks

Large-scale compulsory purchase was seen as a prerequisite for city renewal even when houses were structurally sound and there was strong local resistance (Crossman, 1975). Millions of unmodernised Victorian and Edwardian terraces were targeted by government. Some escaped and were modernised, many did not (Ferris, 1972).

New housing estates were reserved for the victims of clearance, the 'slum dwellers'. The slow emptying, boarding up and disconnection of services turned previously thriving, if poor, neighbourhoods into a sea of dereliction (Hamilton, 1976; Konttinen, 1983). In other European cities, demolition was much more selective and more mixed-use neighbourhoods have survived (Power, 1993).

The forced rupture of old neighbourhoods was occasionally fought off (Hamilton, 1976). But, on the whole, the 'Family and Kinship' story was replayed in maybe 5,000 compact inner city neighbourhoods, as established social networks were destroyed and forced communities in new areas often failed to take root (Wilmott and Young, 1957). Large tracts of inner Liverpool, Manchester, Birmingham, Newcastle, Glasgow, Tower Hamlets and other urban centres were virtually wiped out between 1955 and 1975. Nearly five million people were compulsorily moved (Halsey, 1988). Liverpool lost one-third of its population in the process. Birmingham had a continuous clearance area of 35,000 properties.

The idea that people could be reordered out of slums into new estates did not work. Government took no responsibility for the social upheavals and dislocation that inner city demolition and rebuilding caused (CHAC, 1949, 1953a, 1953b 1955a, 1955b, 1956, 1959, 1969; HSAG, 1978). The informal networks of support that are well documented in low income settlements world-wide were swept away and it took years to rebuild them (Habitat, 1996; Young and Lemos, 1997).

Surplus estates

Estates appeared – sometimes almost end on end as in Tower Hamlets, Southwark, north Lambeth, south Hackney, inner Liverpool, the East End of Newcastle. Many of these new council areas had become hard to let by the early 1970s (DoE, 1974). The Government was first alerted to the problem when councils began advertising vacancies. There were boarded up flats on many large, difficult to let London estates – the GLC advertised in the *Evening Standard* and let over the counter (GLC, 1979; DoE, 1981a). Islington had several estates where it simply couldn't find families to move in (Hamilton, 1976). Demolition of structurally sound blocks began and continues today.

The problem was much more severe in the North. Newcastle forecast in 1976 that it would have a surplus of council housing by 1983 if it kept building (DoE, 1981a). Gateshead councillors in 1975 recommended a halt to council building but the recommendation was rejected for fear of being overtaken by neighbouring local authorities. Liverpool, Birkenhead, Knowsley, Wigan, Blackburn, Oldham, Rochdale and many other areas reported serious demand problems by 1980. Lewisham council in London declared it had enough council housing in 1976 (DoE, 1981a).

By 1980, over half the housing stock of most inner London boroughs and nearly half the stock in most major cities was council-owned and rented. Councils came to dominate cities in a way that had not been clearly foreseen and was unique in Western Europe (Power, 1993).

Estate management

The lack of management structure or expertise in running the now publicly owned areas led to major gaps (DoE, 1981a). For example, the police did not accept responsibility for patrolling estates as 'private areas with unadopted roads' (Islington Borough Council, 1976). Council housing management was not regulated, unlike other public services, and the resulting standards were very poor (CHAC, 1969; HSAG, 1978; Glasgow District Council , 1986). The management task was made much harder as new generations began to grow up in workless households (DoE, 1981b). The derelict docks, warehouses, factories, terminals all now blighted the very estates that they had generated in their heyday.

Bias to renovation

By 1974, under pressure of growing objections, a shortage of suitable sites and cost, few new clearance areas were being announced. Renovation restored some of the popularity of old inner areas. In the early 1980s, it was easier to let a *Coronation Street* house than a brand new flat in Liverpool (DoE, 1981a). In Islington, the shift away from demolition saved many condemned Georgian squares from the bulldozer and drew in younger households who otherwise would not have stayed in inner London. The housing was cheap, accessible and far more spacious than modern 'rabbit hutches' and it became highly attractive (Ferris, 1972). This movement gradually spread across inner London and other cities. Glasgow began to recognise the intrinsic value of its old tenements (Donnison and Middleton, 1987).

Government funding shifted in favour of inner city renewal. But, in spite of General Improvement Areas (1969), Housing Action Areas (1974) and Urban Development Corporations (1981), all aimed at restoring cities, the decline continued. Rather than too little, too late, the rescue of cities was a long-term project in the face of radical economic and social transformations.

Global shifts

International competition, the freeing up of markets and investment led to the collapse of ailing British industries – textiles, steel, coal, shipbuilding, car manufacture and many others. Cities like Manchester and Newcastle were even harder hit in the 1980s by the complex processes of globalisation than in the earlier decades of slow decline (*Economist*, 1998). If public building programmes resembled an unstoppable juggernaut and inner city renewal a stunted Cinderella, economic change was like a tidal wave, swamping whole communities, sweeping away jobs and sucking out the energy and life-blood of whole areas.

The break-up of 'municipal fiefdoms'

The main obsessions of the 1980s became the expansion of owner occupation and the reduction in the scale and power of urban local authority landlords (Forrest and Murie, 1988). The hope was that a more private, more competitive orientation would generate more enterprise. Government policy did not ignore cities, even though councils were no longer the main house builders, nor the principle regenerators (Robson, 1995).

Michael Heseltine's attempt to entice private investors back into inner cities after the Brixton and Toxteth riots met with a luke-warm response. Government had to pump-prime virtually all the new inner city housing, renovation of older property and the infrastructure for inner city renewal (Audit Commission, 1989). Tenants' disillusionment with conditions was used as a weapon to lever change out of local authorities, although this sometimes backfired as in the case of the first Housing Action Trusts (Malpass and Means, 1993).

Throughout the 1980s and 1990s, a battery of initiatives was tried – at one point, there were a dozen simultaneously targeted at inner cities. Most had some impact on conditions. In particular, the Urban Development Corporations, one for every major city, created flagship centre city renewal projects that began to attract new jobs and new residents. They are an interesting case of mixed use, mixed funding partnerships which cities over time came to be proud of. But they were too glamorous and too expensive for poorer and more extensive inner neighbourhoods.

Rescuing estates

Estate Action targeted repair and environmental funds at about 500 estates. Housing associations were encouraged to build new and infill schemes in place of local authorities. But no coherent or concentrated action was taken over the long-run decline of inner neighbourhoods until City Challenge was launched with the return of the hard-hitting Heseltine to attack multiple and highly resistant problems with multiple action (DoE, 1996). In spite of significant visible impacts, under 30 areas were in the programme; they were short-lived (five years) and therefore insufficient to turn the tide in the areas we visited.

The last major Conservative initiative was to pool all city programmes, distribute the money as widely as possible through the Single Regeneration Budget and thereby lower the priority given to cities. This lower commitment was linked with rumbling disorder in many estates and inner areas. In the early 1990s, there were over a hundred disturbances and at least 28 riots, mainly outside London and the South East. There was a clear link between loss of work, loss of a male breadwinner role, aggressive male behaviour and weak policing (see Power and Tunstall, 1997 for further discussion). These riots were local affairs, provoking no inquiry and no new policies. Among the most severe were the riots in Greater Manchester (Salford) and Newcastle.

The numbers game

Meanwhile, house building continued. Housing associations entered their fastest growth period, mainly new stock in inner city estates where it was cheap. Government targets encouraged the numbers game and economies of scale encouraged estates. Lower costs encouraged allocations of funds to the North and the spectacle of unwanted new developments in many northern inner cities began.

Throughout the 1980s and 1990s, between 150,000 and 200,000 new homes a year were built, mostly for owner occupation, mostly outside the cities on greenfield sites, possibly staying slightly ahead of the rate of household formation (House of Commons, 1998).

Councils had undergone 20 years of harsh, negative, downward pressures. Their status and their estates were often in bottom place. In big cities, where municipal landlords were most dominant and in deepest trouble, the knock-on effects on the city as a whole were significant (Pacione, 1997).

By 1995, there were constant press reports of vandals destroying newly built, unoccupied houses, of half-empty estates, of demolition decisions and of plummeting demand (see Appendix 8). Table 36 shows how these broad societal and economic changes affected low income neighbourhoods, fuelling the urban exodus.

Table 36 Impacts of wider changes on local neighbourhoods

Wider urban and societal changes ⟷	Local inner city and neighbourhood changes
Industrial decline/job change	Highly concentrated impacts of large-scale changes
City exodus and North/South drift	Acute poverty and job losses
Decline in social housing popularity	Council estates become stigmatised
Clustering of problems	Empty property
Lower standards of service	High turnover
Falling densities	Low value property
Declining reputation of cities	Lower entry requirements
Interlocking problems	'Left behind' population
Poor schools, security, environment	High unemployment/low skill
Rising demand in more popular areas	Plummeting demand and abandonment in unpopular areas
Settlements leapfrog beyond urban fringe	Local controls deteriorate
Anti-urban bias	Neighbourhoods caught in vicious spiral
Feeds neighbourhood decline	Feeds anti-urban prejudice

12 Driving factors

There are three main pressures militating against the survival of the poorest neighbourhoods including the four we studied:

- first, the intense social and economic polarisation of the poorest areas leading to the prospect of chaotic conditions, as happened on some council estates in the 1970s, 1980s and 1990s (Power, 1997; Power and Tunstall, 1997)

- second, the dominance of council ownership in cities and the mismatch between area tenure and the strong aspiration to choose and to own

- third, the strong lure of suburban and relatively low cost owner occupation leading those who can buy to abandon poor inner neighbourhoods and fuelling the exodus.

The social face of cities has been gradually transformed (CPRE, 1998; Rudlin, 1998). The people left behind in the process, descendants of traditional working class communities and newcomers to the urban scene, occupy old neighbourhoods that have become all but unrecognisable. Table 37 illustrates the push and pull factors. Figure 7 illustrates the long pattern of urban decline.

Both Manchester and Newcastle have been hard hit by sprawling greenfield building. Yet 'land is a finite resource and we cannot afford to be profligate with it' (Raynsford, 1999). It is still cheaper and easier to use greenfield than recycled inner city land. However, if the full infrastructure, social and economic costs of greenfield development were included, brownfields would be more attractive.

No government department is responsible for monitoring the building targets that are being set or the planning permissions that are being allowed. Unitary Development Plans, produced by every local authority, are not scrutinised for consistency. Nor are they regularly updated. The statement within Newcastle's Plan that the city still suffers from housing shortages and too high density contradicts available evidence (Newcastle City Council, 1998c, DETR, 1998b).

We now link the pressures and trends we have explored to the experience of our inner neighbourhoods. The factors affecting them are grouped under six main headings.

Table 37 Push and pull factors in the abandonment of inner neighbourhoods

Push factors	Pull factors
Unpopularity – low value	Desire to upgrade
Poor services, particularly education	Escape from inner city
Accelerated decay	High premium on security
Unpredictability	Desire for peaceful environment
Demoralisation, despair	Pro-suburban bias
Low income/poverty	Higher value neighbourhoods
Sense of loss of control – insecurity	Affordability – cheap owner occupation
Aggressive, disruptive behaviour	Ready supply outside cities

Figure 7 Cumulative urban decline leading to collapse in neighbourhood conditions

City decline

↓

Exit of skilled population

↓

Growing poverty, de-skilling

↓

Suburban owner occupation gets cheaper – more space – better amenities

↓

Social housing stock continues to expand (to 1993)

↓

Estates lose popularity

↓

Poorest estates become marginal

↓

Politicians 'in denial' – inadequate response

↓

Worst areas damage city image

↓

Greenfield developments to hold population

↓

Inner areas collapse

Source: Based on European Urban programmes; Power, 1993.

Reputation

The reputation and history of the areas brought with them lasting problems. From the outside, the old slum areas were stereotyped as crime-ridden, ignorant and unruly (Wohl, 1977). Much of this reputation carried over into the council estates that replaced them (DoE, 1981a). As times changed, people sought constantly to leave, upgrade and improve. Thus, tied into the history of poverty was a history of instability.

Poor areas often had a much more positive side – a strong sense of 'community' in the old-fashioned sense, gritty almost defiant pride in what had been the very base of England's industrial wealth. Difficult conditions generated an instinct for survival and close family networks (see case studies). These positive elements helped people to cope with the struggle at the bottom but they did not overcome the harsh industrial legacy. The sense of solidarity within the community was often an attempt to fight back at a social order that relied on large groups being at or near the bottom. Overall, the lowest income communities were battling with weak rather than strong levers. This was accentuated as traditional institutions such as unions, churches and friendly societies lost members and their cutting edge (Thompson, 1990). The transformation of work, requiring different and higher skills, has reinforced this problem, making much traditional education in low income areas unprepared and as yet unable to generate new standards and skills sufficiently fast (Blunkett, 1998).

As neighbourhoods shrank and lost their employment base, so the negative image of an area became stronger, generating a sense of shame. It is easy to become depressed when the rationale for a community is lost – 'when work disappears', and conditions deteriorate (Wilson, 1997). Thus, history and reputation become attached to the people who are identified with an area and its problems (Gauldie, 1979).

In spite of this, some residents were deeply committed to their neighbourhoods working tirelessly for the good of the community. They had not given up hope, but they recognised the downward pressures on their neighbourhoods. In particular, they were distressed by the negative behaviour of many younger residents and some families. They felt this compounded the poor reputation and betrayed all they struggled for:

One or two kids were holding the estate to ransom and it got a bad name. It crept up on us. (Resident, City-Edge)

Housing and environmental conditions

The economy, housing and environment interact strongly but with a time lag. As jobs go, so people filter out to new housing built in growth areas. More anchored and traditional residents often do not want to go. The environment decays as economic shifts continue, creating a sense of dereliction.

There is a singular absence of any overall environmental plan for the areas. It is the confusion of open spaces, derelict land, empty buildings, lack of trees, loss of an ordered sense of urbanity that so stigmatises the most abandoned areas, making them look uncared for, unvalued and unwanted.

Regeneration initiatives definitely improve the image of the targeted areas by upgrading the environment, but often they are too short-term, too capital intensive and too disruptive of the existing population, leading to further population movement (see case studies) and an abrupt loss of momentum at the end of each specific programme (Robson, 1995).

Areas need long-term management of conditions, with people on the ground constantly checking, supervising, mending, clearing, guarding, controlling, linking, listening. Little of this activity is funded through programmes of intervention, or through local authority mainstream services. Earlier studies have highlighted this need (Carley and Kirk, 1998; Gregory, 1998).

Overall, there is far too strong an emphasis on physical regeneration and building, and too little sense of what might make areas 'tick' again. The truth must lie in some combination of physical and social spending, capital and revenue programmes.

Empty demolition sites, empty
council homes and empty shops

Building for a surplus or gentrification?

Neighbourhood abandonment leads to a fight to counter the decline. Hence, new, low cost housing is going up in the very streets that have been cleared for lack of demand. No one yet knows whether the new housing will take root and new residents will stay. But only by stemming the wider flow out of cities will demand for these areas rise again. This has not yet begun to happen.

There are some hopeful signs. Better quality housing close to the city centres is selling better than predicted and there appears to be demand for more (Manchester and Newcastle, 1998; Rudlin, 1998.) Appealing to higher income, younger working households with new-style city flats and town houses offers one way forward for areas that are quite literally abandoned by traditional employers and residents. The quayside along the Tyne is rapidly being claimed by developers on the back of the Urban Development Corporation's investment in the 1980s/90s (Newcastle City Council, 1998b). The old warehouses of central Manchester offer spacious and attractive 'loft apartments' that are selling for 40 times the price of a terraced house only a mile away. (Manchester City Council, 1998d). These high quality developments are having a knock-on effect on the image of city housing and on the standard of services offered.

The benefits have not yet hit the neighbourhoods we studied, but they are sometimes only minutes away and they symbolise a shift in thinking. What was formerly rejected as a hated industrial relic is being 'gentrified'. Developers are building modest but attractive homes for young incomers in two of the neighbourhoods creating the beginning of more mixed, more

balanced areas. Trickle down theories are strongly disputed but cities are dynamic vehicles and the direction of change does affect both poor and rich. The new dynamics may be more pro-city and therefore indirectly pro-poor. The involvement of private as well as public partners signals the new opportunities (Urban Splash, 1998).

Management pressures

The management problems generated by conditions of incipient abandonment are little short of overwhelming. Some councils, after years of over-bureaucratic, rule-bound, procedure-driven systems, are ready to push out all the boats in precarious neighbourhoods. Local staff, local offices, local lettings and resident links are now commonplace in more go-ahead areas in response to the real urgency. However, these moves are often not backed by localised budgets, direct control over service delivery or sufficient local decision-making powers (Power and Tunstall, 1995). The management structures are often not strong enough to stem the tide. As a result, really radical experiments only rarely emerge.

However, tough enforcement on crime and anti-social behaviour appears to be having some effect. The introduction of concierges into blocks of flats is restoring viability to some previously half-empty blocks. Localised staff appear to contain spiralling conditions and win some battles (see case studies). But, unless there is more demand, management energies may be leeched away. One of the requirements of successful management is to get many elements right together (Power, 1997; Gregory, 1998; Social Exclusion Unit, 1998). Management only works over small areas, yet a co-ordinated effort

Quayside development, Newcastle upon Tyne

REVITALISING INNER CITIES
Source: Urban splash

Britannia Basin, Manchester

Old Haymarket, Liverpool

over large areas is essential. Getting this combination of highly localised inputs and broader city strategies to work together is highly elusive. Both Manchester and Newcastle are battling with these dilemmas (see Appendices 6 and 7).

Disrupted communities

Social problems dominate the consciousness of all who live and work in inner neighbourhoods. Tenants are constantly trying to move away from the edges of estates where they might be exposed and vulnerable, or the middle where they might feel trapped and forgotten. Thus, strips of empty property keep growing. Many people – residents and staff – talked about the problems at night when no one was around. People referred to gangs, criminals and rough behaviour. This sense of dread is real, but it is difficult to judge how many people are involved – probably a small minority, even though it is sufficiently aggressive to swamp counter trends:

There is a massive problem with an over-supply of housing. It has wrecked communities. They are now unsustainable. This part of the city is just a choice of bad areas to live in.
(Former HA development worker, Bankside)

One explanation for the growth of neighbour nuisance and behaviour breakdown is the growing concentration of difficult people in a shrinking stock of public housing. A single family can wreak havoc where there is space in which to operate:

One 'wrong' person moves into a street, and the whole street empties. The perpetrator stays, the victim moves. (Resident, Bankside)

Abandonment and high turnover make that minority even more conspicuous. In the control vacuum that often arises as the stable population declines, behaviour that might have been contained spills over:

We had eight abandonments in the course of three to four weeks. Five of those were on the same street and were mainly to do with this problem family vandalising the area and threatening people. They were wrecking our properties as they became empty. So we had to put up screening which made the street look worse. Even then, they were pulling the front porches off and setting fire to the gas meters. One tenant has had bricks thrown through her window. Members of this family have punched people in the street.
(Housing association officer, City-Edge)

Disruptive behaviour like this affects local schools. Some children react aggressively to the violence and destruction they see around them.

Other social problems are quieter – low income, lack of work, lone parenthood, for example. But they actually feed into disorder at the extreme, because residents have fewer resources, lower morale, weaker links and less back-up with which to make things work. They also become depressed more easily and depression readily converts into aggression – particularly among young men.

It appears impossible to sustain social cohesion when large areas have become almost universally poor in a wider context of growing affluence. Both cities advocate an income and social mix within the inner city as the only effective counter to the mounting social problems (Manchester and Newcastle, 1998). Residents often agree:

Some people think you should just start all over again and attract in much higher income people who could make it work. (Resident, Bankside)

But spreading rather than concentrating problems is easier said than done. New supports and new initiatives to integrate marginal households have to be constantly created (Shelter, 1998). Manchester's original strategy to combat anti-social behaviour in council housing through evictions, injunctions, witness support and other enforcement mechanisms is both popular and contentious. On the ground, it is strongly defended. Enforcement often leads to improvement. The signals sent out by setting clear boundaries can contain behaviour.

Cumulative crisis

We observed the phenomenon of 'tipping' from viability to unviability as areas go into a steep slide and problems reach breaking point. Some parts of all four areas became unsaveable. The key measures of tipping were zero demand, property abandonment and the decision to allow demolition by managers and residents. Power, energy, resources and authority all become so depleted that, over a short period, many elements of viability collapse. No one any longer has a grip on conditions. Figure 8 summarises the process of 'tipping'.

Figure 8 Tipping point in neighbourhood decline

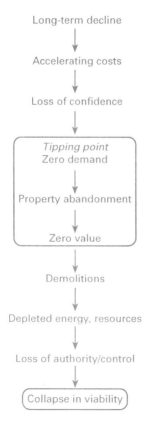

Part V
A way forward

The measures we found in place often countered or slowed the downward trends and in some areas seemed to contain the worst problems:

Our residents' association was set up because we wanted to tackle what we saw as the area being left to deteriorate. I decided that the area was worth fighting for. (Resident, City-Edge)

No one agency has the answer or the capability to deal with the problem ... it's so massive that we all need to work together.
(Secondary school head, Bankside)

Table 38 summarises those micro-actions that cumulatively prevented the collapse that many feared.

Social exclusion

The term was invented in France in the early 1980s to describe people cut off from work and other support. It has become a catch-all phrase for poverty and related social problems. It resonates in Britain where polarisation increased rapidly in the 1980s (Joseph Rowntree Foundation, 1995). Social exclusion has quickly risen to the top of the political agenda.

New patterns of work are driving these changes in post-industrial economies (Reich, 1993; Marris, 1996; Wilson, 1996). Older industrial centres are harder hit than more diverse, service-based, 'modern' areas (Jargowsky, 1997). But, in Britain, all large cities and most sizeable towns experience problems of social exclusion. It is a product of many pressures and changes working together to push more disadvantaged people to the edge of society, often preventing them from partici-pating and depriving them of opportunity. The least popular council estates and poor inner cities are particularly strongly affected because of their historic role in housing a manual workforce (Social Exclusion Unit, 1998). There is no one pattern of decline, as some cities and areas have coped and responded better than others.

Social exclusion is associated with the ghettoisation of people and areas. Tackling inner city problems and rebuilding cities more generally is a key to creating social cohesion because pro-urban policies work against the development of social ghettos.

We have a strong legacy of universal underpinning through the Welfare State in education, health and social security. This underpinning is still remarkably intact (Hills, 1998). It provides vital bridges between all areas and all citizens. Area programmes depend on them. The new government is targeting the most deprived areas with intense initiatives based on universal programmes. New ideas draw on earlier experience of successful regeneration (Robson, 1995; DETR 1998c, 1998d). This should help inner city neighbourhoods.

Many of the new government Action Zones, the emphasis on education and health, the crime and disorder measures, the supportive approach to families, and targeting the worst areas through New Deal for Communities are designed to combat social exclusion (Prime Minister, 1998). The bundle of benefit and tax reforms announced by the Chancellor in 1998 helps to move low income households closer to solvency and in the direction of integration (Hills, 1998). While these measures are national policies, they are applied regionally and locally to create local responsive programmes.

Table 38 Local action in four neighbourhoods to hold conditions[1]

Housing	Residents	Police/security	Schools	Health
Local office	Residents' and tenants' associations	Local policing	Breakfast clubs	Resource centre
Local lettings	Homewatch projects	Special liaison with residents	Lunch-time clubs	Local pharmacy
Screening lettings	Links with police	Liaison with other services	Parent involvement	Health project including group for stroke patients and their carers
Flexible letting, e.g. under-occupy	Credit union	Witness support	Adult education	Mental health awareness training for front-line staff
Concierge in tower blocks	Community development	Community safety strategy	Anti-truancy measures	Support group for drug users
Furnished tenancies	Monitoring housing and environmental services	Youth initiatives, e.g. volunteer cadet force, school links, diversionary work	Anti-bullying measures	**Special resources**
Estate agreements	Input into allocations	Target-hardening	Improvements to school buildings	Estate Action
Advertising	Negotiating estate improvement	Closed circuit television	Extra inputs for transition from primary to secondary	City Challenge
Selective demolition	Assistance in securing empties	Crime patterns analysis	Parent links	Single Regeneration Budget
Modernisation	Campaign for introductory tenancies	Safer Estates initiative	Welfare support	New Deal for Communities
Lighting		Arson task force	**Employment[3]**	
Fencing	**Voluntary organisations[2]**	Security project including patrols by guards	Training, skills, development	**Cross-service working**
External upgrading	Settlement		Outreach	Community planning
Landscaping of cleared sites	Church action		Job link/job search/job preparation	Policing with housing staff and residents
Estate remodelling	Neighbourhood watch		Work experience	Child supervision
Tenure diversification	Community security projects		Employer links	Family support
Engaging private landlords	Community Trust		Compacts	Anti-social behaviour
LA securing private empties	Housing co-operative		Inward investment/new jobs	
Action on enforcement	Community centre			
Link to employment	Food co-operative			
Multi-landlord links				

1 Not all action is taken in all four neighbourhoods.
2 Other voluntary organisations are listed under other headings.
3 Often insufficient local targeting.

Table 39 summarises the programmes, powers and proposals for tackling urban and neighbourhood problems currently in train. They are divided between national, regional, district and neighbourhood policies and approaches. At neighbourhood level a clear framework does not yet exist (see section on 'Neighbourhood management or strategic vision?' later in this chapter).

Marketing social housing

Social landlords so dominate rental housing in cities that a broad strategy of rehousing varied social groups is vital in helping cities to recover. Cohesion depends on a sense of belonging, links between neighbours, support networks and informal controls (Young and Lemos, 1997). Most people attach high importance to living in 'a good area'. These essentials become elusive when only the people with the least resources and most difficulties are rehoused together in a small area without intensive support, particularly when there is a sense of coercion and loss of control.

The strict emphasis on rehousing tenants according to need has destroyed the social viability of much council housing and may do the same for housing associations. It has also over time excluded people who might want to rent and who would stay in cities if they could.

The problem of needs-based allocations as the only access route to estates is recognised across the country. Our evidence shows that the result is lettings problems in high pressure areas like London as well as the Midlands, West and North (see Appendix 1).

As demand for social renting has fallen,

there is a golden opportunity to try new approaches. Active marketing of good quality, relatively cheap housing attracts a broader range of applicants than are currently considered eligible (GLC, 1979). It will make difficult to let but good condition areas more popular as long as many other external and local supports are in place. This approach was successful in the 1980s in some of the most difficult estates (Power, 1984, 1991b). It is unlikely to attract more than a few affluent applicants. But about half the population should be eligible on a broader definition of need.

Access can be organised on continental lines to help ensure a greater social mix. In Denmark, anyone who wants to can apply for social housing and a strong mixture is encouraged in order to retain public support and prevent 'ghettos' of poor people. A quarter of lettings go to emergencies. In Germany, a majority rent; about 60 per cent of the population is eligible for 'social' housing, a loose term for all subsidised housing. In France, some social housing is targeted at acute need, but a majority is for moderate income households looking for a home, a very general interpretation of need (Power, 1993). In Holland, all social lettings are advertised to ensure broad access on the assumption that many people want an affordable home in cities near work. Manchester is currently advertising widely for its whole stock. Within steeply declining neighbourhoods, advertising among relatives, friends and others connected with the area is often a crucial first step. Some previously unpopular tower blocks in the neighbourhoods have been successfully filled through advertising coupled with special security and screening measures.

Table 39 Different levels of government programmes, powers and proposals linked to disadvantaged areas

National	Regional	District	Neighbourhood
Pro-city programmes	Regional economic development	Representative democracy	Neighbourhood co-ordination
Brownfield focus	Development plans	Local government	Neighbourhood management
Urban transport	Green belt protection	Economic development	Local housing management
Universal underpinning	City development	Service co-ordination and strategic vision for district	Local policing and security
• Education	Regeneration programmes	Local conditions and standards	Local environmental maintenance
• Health	Regional co-ordination and representation	Best value implementation	Open spaces
• Social security	Resource distribution	Local environmental protection	Local schools and school liaison – play centres, community, adult, parent support
• Public infrastructure and services	Regional transport	Enforcement	Other support services, e.g. social services
• New Deal for Work	Regional change, housing investment and planning, etc.	Responsibility for education, other services	Youth work and adult education
Redistributive grant to local authorities for urban services	Administrative arm of government	Child care/social services	Leisure activities, holiday programmes, after school activities
Special initiatives	• Standards	Strategic input into police and health authorities	Nurseries and child care delivery
• SRB	• Environment	Crime audit	Resident consultation and involvement/liaison
• Action Zones	• Targeting	Traffic and transport	Estate agreements/tenant management/estate forums
– Education	Land use, recycling, brownfield strategy	Local development plan	Multi-service partnership
– Health	Training and enterprise development	Brownfield target delivery	Enforcement of standards
– Employment	Regional Development Agencies	Ownership and management of council housing	Local delivery point for all services and programmes
• Sure Start	Expanded regional government (Scotland, Wales, Northern Ireland, potentially English regions)	Allocation of council housing and nominations to housing association developments	
• New Deal for Communities		Stock transfer	
Legislative reform proposals		Regeneration strategy	
• Local government		Partnerships in special programmes	
• Crime and disorder		Private sector liaison	
Social Exclusion Unit			
• Rough sleeping			
• Truancy and school exclusion			
• Disadvantaged neighbourhoods			
• Young, lone parents			

Table 39 Different levels of government programmes, powers and proposals linked to disadvantaged areas (continued)

National	Regional	District	Neighbourhood
Policy Action Teams addressing disadvantaged areas Pressures on performance • Best value • Audit commission regulation/inspection Environmental agenda	Police and health authorities (often organised above local authority level)	Local Agenda 21 Front line for local government initiatives Zones Crime prevention Pro-city and pro-neighbourhood plans Anti-poverty and inclusion Local consultation Neighbourhood initiatives	Geographical location for most special initiatives Targeting mechanism Neighbourhood and community plans Local regeneration initiatives

Note: Many of these proposals are not yet ready for implementation, particularly at neighbourhood level.

An obvious argument against open lettings is that they might create more homelessness. Squeezing needy households, however, in the eyes of potential and existing residents, raises the value of social housing which is a prerequisite for making estates work.

It is possible to reserve up to half of new lettings for social housing for emergencies in order to prevent homelessness whilst the rest can be let through a constantly updated, open date order queue without the discretion, discrimination and sense of coercion that attaches to 'merit' systems, such as points. This approach was recommended 30 years ago in the government review of council housing allocations by Cullingworth, but was never implemented, a tragedy of short-sightedness from which council housing never recovered (Cullingworth, 1969). Cullingworth's committee stressed fairness, equal access, an open system and the avoidance of ghettos.

Mechanisms are necessary to ensure access to better property for lower income households and to prevent higher income groups benefiting from windfall gains. Restrictions would be necessary to prevent Right to Buy profiteering, inherited secure tenancies and unfair priority for the most sought after properties. Table 40 outlines some positive and negative lettings mechanisms.

A second argument is that the government should not subsidise better-off tenants to live in low rent council homes. But the counter-argument is that working rent payers will help to keep up the value and viability of social housing. More housing demand will create more competition, and put different pressures on landlords and tenants. But some households in work have been unnecessarily put off renting, and social renting in particular, creating wider pressures and costs exemplified by urban sprawl. The positive effects may far outweigh the negative and the alternative of allowing areas of exclusively low income housing to be progressively abandoned, even by needy households, is the most damaging and expensive option of all. This is happening nationwide (Power and Mumford report to the Housing Corporation, 1999).

Allocating housing without choice to the poorest people fits uneasily with modern urban society. It creates a high refusal and dissatisfaction rate. Restrictive, narrowly needs-based allocations, particularly one offer only to homeless families, causes an increase in refusals and a higher level of empty property. This approach has been most damaging in large flatted estates. The level of empty property in some London boroughs has been exceptionally high because of this failure (Power and Tunstall, 1997). Less precarious tenants are needed to create more mixed, stable estates. There is the space in less popular areas to do it, *but* social housing generally should be opened up in order to ensure its long-term survival. Table 41 suggests some measures to make this work.

Nothing could be more costly than social ghettos as the US experience has demonstrated. They drive away more affluent populations leaving the poorest, most discriminated against people marooned in a sea of dereliction (HUD, 1997; Vergara, 1997). If opening up allocations creates more demand for social housing, then new styles of affordable housing and multiple access routes will have to be invented.

Some people argue that the notion of 'social' housing itself should be abandoned and we should create a more diverse 'regulated rented

Table 40 Lettings approaches

Damaging lettings approaches	Ingredients of open access to social housing
One offer only policies	Open waiting list and letting procedures
Homelessness as dominant access route	All lettings advertised
Opaque points system	Broad eligibility, e.g. below average income
No clear position in queue	Checks on basic eligibility and suitability
No guarantee of reaching top of any list	Date order queue
Member interventions and special pleading	Transparent priority access for emergencies
Lack of internal transfers	Target lettings for clear priorities, e.g. statutory homeless
Unaccompanied viewings	Clear, simple definition of need
Poor cleaning and redecorating of property on offer	Careful management of lettings in precarious areas
Lack of local 'settling' support	No Right to Buy for new tenants in high demand areas
No clear control over impact of lettings on specific areas	Payment of nominal administration fee (similar to college applications)
	Automatic annual update deleting non-respondents
	Discretionary restrictions to prevent abuse
	Special support mechanisms for rehousing vulnerable families
	Special housing provisions for special needs households
	Open transfer system in date order queuing
	Simple eligibility requirements for transfer of clean rent record and property conditions
	Local control over matching of applicant and dwelling
	Personalised introduction to tenancy
	Clear, simple tenancy conditions
	Settling in via local office, super-caretaking

sector'. This implies the continued transfer of council housing to 'registered social landlords' to encourage more diversity, investment, resident commitment and business management. An obvious first step is to move housing ownership and management out of the political arena, so that all landlords have an incentive to run their housing as a long-term asset (DETR, 1998e).

Regeneration

Targeting 'worst first' is normal regeneration practice because the worst areas blight surroundings, destroying urban environments and reputations. Some areas may eventually become redundant and demolition becomes inevitable, but this has to happen within a broader strategy of holding conditions in

Table 41 Landlord mechanisms for retaining residents and attracting incomers in low demand areas

Management mechanisms	Linking with residents
Strong local presence	Careful management of allocations
Well motivated, supervised local staff – at least one per 100 rented dwellings	– Relaxed approach to transfers within area
	– Support for rehousing relatives and locally connected applicants
Immediate action on basic conditions – cleaning, repair, wear and tear	– Resident liaison
Consistent legal enforcements against criminal activity	Systematic consultation over problems and priorities
Meticulous attention to detail – highly localised responses	– Constantly adapting actions
	– Constant feedback on progress
Day to day liaison and reporting between residents and staff	– Priorities in liaison with residents
	– Local improvement budgets
Special management measures to support new lettings initiatives, e.g. students, flat sharers, elderly	Special initiatives with partners
	– To engage and involve young people
	– To build skills and generate jobs particularly among younger residents
Links between open marketing and local lettings	– To support families in difficulty
	– To integrate different groups
Close liaison with police, education, social services, youth, environmental services	Gradual improvements and upgrading
	– Medium- and long-term plan for overall rescue
Intensive caretaking of large blocks, e.g. towers and general environmental care	– Neighbourhood management
	– Revenue resources

precarious areas. This means planning and spreading capital investment, repair and environmental care across inner cities, not just within short-term regeneration programmes. Recognition of long-term needs is provoking stock transfer plans in many cities. These now play a growing part in regeneration (DETR, 1998c).

Regeneration can work only in the context of winning back more people in work and with higher skills – they are essential to neighbourhood vitality, entrepreneurship and investment. The need for local services to meet their aspirations in turn generates mixed uses. Work then begins to find its way into the pattern of neighbourhood recovery. The transitions of the post-industrial era are already creating many new style jobs which lower skilled people can do (Sassen, 1998).

The quayside developments in Newcastle and the canalside warehouse conversions in Manchester, levered into existence with regeneration funds, demonstrate this new urban approach (DoE, 1997). It is unlikely to be true that lower income households are excluded from the benefits of these developments, but proactive local and national governments help ensure inclusion.

Crucial to the success of regeneration is developing basic skills and capacity building among local residents. Most regeneration programmes recognise this (DETR, 1998c,

1998d). It is a subtle and often elusive task requiring highly localised and sensitive inputs (Richardson, 1997).

To do all this requires a strongly led local authority, less involved in hands-on detail, more dynamic in promoting neighbourhoods, partnerships, local regeneration companies and new initiatives. The public landlord role may act as a barrier to fast change. Table 42 shows how successful regeneration projects evolve.

Some regeneration will happen on its own in more desirable areas but most needs pump-priming, social infrastructure and environmental upgrading. There is a strong link between city-wide planning, resource allocation and neighbourhood action. Most importantly, the brownfields focus will work only in an even playing field.

Interestingly, developers are ahead of the game – pioneering core city conversions, proposing inner renewal schemes and capitalising on untapped demand from higher income groups to return to the city. They rely on pro-city investment from national, regional and local government. In Manchester and Newcastle, developers are actively looking for opportunities within regeneration programmes such as New Deal for Communities (Newcastle City Council, 1998f). Lenders need to be drawn in behind this new interest in regeneration (National House-Building Council Conference, 1998). Newcastle's challenged appeal to the government to build executive homes in the green belt may falter. The infrastructure costs to the city are huge and developers may be willing to consider expanding outwards from the successful city centre developments, as an alternative to developing beyond the city's outer ring (Newcastle City Council, 1998d,

1998e, 1998f).

Housing associations are heavily involved in regeneration already as our case studies show. They can borrow to upgrade existing local authority stock under transfer to new company-style structures. Associations have to take much of the financial risk, alongside private developers, if they want to build new housing. But they can help to renew and diversify inner areas; particularly estates crying out for investment.

In spite of the emergence of 'gated communities' in the United States, with some pale imitations in Britain, cities as well as villages thrive on mixture. It is one of the most attractive aspects of city life that people of many different backgrounds and experiences share a common space. Making those common spaces work is a central role of civic society.

The government has tried many routes to regeneration over three decades. The experience gives us clues to successful ingredients, many of which are built into the new regeneration programmes, as Figure 9 summarises (Robson, 1995; DETR, 1998c, 1998d).

Holding on to residents

Residents who have put up with so much should benefit from any gains of regeneration. This is central to social cohesion. Constantly dispersing communities undermines the possibility of restoring a sense of neighbourhood, and residents who understand how things happen locally are a strong guide to priorities.

Holding on to long-standing residents helps to stabilise rapidly declining areas. A clean sweep fits ill with the more successful city

Table 42 Stages in developing neighbourhood and district regeneration strategies

Identify broad problems	Overview of local, city-wide and regional problems Community and political pressures Select target areas
Collect evidence	Press reports History of area Official and local reports, meetings, Census, records
Analyse problems and possibilities	Bite-sized steps Think the unthinkable
Plan action	Target specific areas Cost options Set out timetable Designate pump-priming budget Identify troubleshooter
Negotiate partners	Responsibilities Written agreements Leadership
Identify resources	Bid for cash Minimum/maximum requirements Internal/external bidding
Revamp plan	Options in light of resources Baseline plan for the neighbourhood management Allow for variations
Identify delivery team	Functions, goals, powers, responsibilities
Appoint 'supremo'	To fill in detail To chase delivery To lead implementation To clarify decision making To appoint board
Appoint board	Balanced representation Resident involvement Strong independent chair
Move to action	Identify fast, deliverable targets Consult widely in area Recruit local steering group
Focus on resident priorities	Core problems – caretaking, etc. Skills/job links Youth/police/schools Training, employment
Monitor activity/spending/results	Local information Resident input
Evaluate	Adjust plan Introduce new ideas
Extend action	Long-term management *not* exit Renegotiate, reallocate, adjust resources

Figure 9 Essential lessons of regeneration

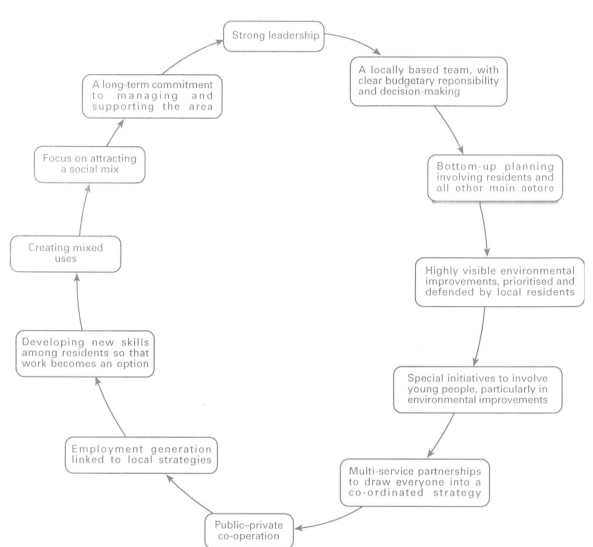

neighbourhoods (Jacobs, 1970). We have argued that the best urban regeneration embodies existing assets within a new dynamism. This was a main lesson from *Estates on the Edge* (Power 1997). Chaotically declining communities were rescued and conditions reversed, with existing residents forming the core of restored communities. Many special supports were introduced to help families in difficulty. Manchester has introduced innovative approaches to this problem. An organic approach, responding to the priorities of stable residents, quelling their fears and meeting their needs, can improve conditions radically. A still occupied area with some slack is easier to develop than an abandoned area where signs abound of complete collapse. Table 43 shows this approach.

Table 43 Organic, incremental regeneration

Action	Implication
Save, reuse and renovate all adaptable buildings	Modify building forms and uses
Avoid large-scale clearances wherever possible	Respond to resident objections to demolitian and amend plans
Avoid random demolition	Restrict demolition to selective blocks or small areas
Involve residents in planning action	Avoid blueprint, open action planning within clear strategy
Constantly amend and adapt plans	Put strong leadership into overall environmental and social planning
Focus on viable communities	Reinforce positive resident action
Work at edges of area – boundaries with better conditions	Build links to centre
Encourage resident involvement	Strong local management
Maximise local back-up services	Give signals of constant care

Density

In British urban history, we confused the poverty and chaos of early urban growth with high density. In order to address poor conditions, we drove our cities outwards. In the mass housing era, we built high-rise blocks in an attempt to reduce overcrowding, create more open space, cope with green belt restrictions and objections to council housing in more conservative suburbs (Dunleavy, 1981). By concentrating poverty within council estates, we combined high rise and high need (Power, 1987). This, coupled with lack of adequate caretaking or guarding, led to rapid decay.

In practice, high quality is often associated with high density. Old crowded neighbourhoods in Rome, Paris, Barcelona, Madrid, Edinburgh are sought after and successful. Population density in Barcelona's inner neighbourhoods is at least ten times higher than in British inner cities (Urban Task Force, 1999a). Georgian terraces in inner London, Glasgow and Amsterdam are very high density.

Higher density is making a comeback (Travers, 1998). When control over entrances is combined with careful allocations, tower blocks prove popular, secure and relatively easy to regenerate. This is drawing public attention (*Guardian*, January 1999).

Smaller households and city exodus mean that less people occupy urban space. It is therefore possible to increase the number of households living in cities without crowding people. Smaller households can be more compactly fitted in, to generate sufficient street life and support services for new housing to really work.

The Joseph Rowntree Foundation's innovative proposals for high density, high quality rented accommodation in central Leeds and Birmingham point to new thinking on densities, single person housing, super-caretaking and city living (Best, 1998). The

Peabody Trust, historically associated with high density and intensive secure management, is pioneering new schemes following this model (Peabody Trust, 1996–98).

A secret of success in creating mixed urban communities is higher density. Social housing can be built into new development invisibly, if we copy the Dutch example of quality design and finish. These new styles rely on choice rather than coercion (National House-Building Council Conference, 1998; Urban Splash, 1998).

High density supports services, street life and interchange. Low density encourages the opposite, a sense of emptiness, a lack of informal controls, an inadequate resource base for essential services and a deep sense of insecurity. Low income makes all these things much worse. Having sufficient people to support shops, to fund custodial caretaking, to use public transport creates informal supervision through street activity. But a combination of neighbourhood management measures is necessary to make density work. The continental model of urban maintenance is far stronger and more effective than British models partly as a result of higher density. It applies in owner occupied as well as rented areas.

The new core city private developments in Manchester and Newcastle are similarly high density, well serviced, environmentally attractive, in strong demand (Manchester City Council, 1998d).

Now is the time to change planning guidelines as a way of enhancing the urban environment, expanding the number of people we can house in cities, reintroducing front-line supervision.

Household size and formation

Eighty-five per cent of all additional households over the next 20 years are projected to be single people. Fifty per cent of them may need affordable housing (Holmans, 1995).

Households are breaking up and reforming in many new ways. This generates some of the projected smaller households, although the elderly form a large proportion of them. But family break-up also creates reconstituted households, pulling many people who become single into new partnerships and cutting-back the rate of household growth. This is one explanation offered in both cities for lower housing demand, less new household formation and higher turnover than expected. It is important, therefore, not to rely too heavily on projections but to look at hard evidence of local demand and need more directly (Keenan, 1998).

Many more single elderly people will require housing within reach of main services in the future. Cities and towns will play a big role. Inventing new housing ideas to help single people feel less isolated and closer to support is critical to social cohesion. Ensuring family-friendly cities is too.

New factors can influence behaviour. For example, commuting becomes less popular as traffic congestion grows. Some working mothers are opting in favour of cities to avoid long-distance commuting and loss of child contact. City centres become more attractive to some childless households as they become more numerous; resistance to building in the countryside grows as more green fields disappear; rebuilding inner neighbourhoods becomes more attractive to the private sector under positive urban management. Household behaviour is already responding to some of these signals as John Prescott's own response to environmental pressures illustrates (DETR, 1998b).

Shrinking household size makes many of the houses and flats we saw standing empty potentially attractive to new households as long as overall environmental security, back-up services and neighbourhood management are provided.

Policing

To win popular support for a return to cities in the face of deep insecurity and long-run decay, more is required than marketing, regeneration and a change in attitude. A prerequisite is a new approach to policing.

One of the reasons for behavioural breakdown is the unequal policing of areas. Weak enforcement highlights this (Power and Tunstall, 1997). Over decades, the police increasingly withdrew into patrol cars and central offices. On the other hand, the police are expected to broker the ills of society without clear rules. In a democracy, we want it both ways – freedom to choose how we live and freedom from the consequences.

Gradually, it is becoming clear that many levels of control by many agencies make for more peaceful communities. Strict enforcement, clear visibility on the streets, constant links with parents, co-operation with other authority figures, a swift response from local organisational bases and immediate action over small transgressions can stem a rising tide of more serious crime. These measures help to create a climate of confidence and security that reinforces people's willingness to step in.

Crucially, positive or proactive policing encourages positive community behaviour.

Many liberals dislike the notion of intensive policing. But, in cities of strangers – which is the essential nature of modern city neighbourhoods – the brokering of law and order by recognised authority figures is a prerequisite for community safety and stability.

Policing difficult neighbourhoods carries many risks and requires skill, continuity and consistency. Young people, particularly young men, react with hostility and aggression to police intervention after they have been allowed to develop law-breaking habits. However, they tend to respect clear rules that allow them the right to be out and about within the bounds of civic responsibility. This is where crowded streets, mixed uses, high density and strong policing can work together. They give youths the right to roam and gather as they have always done, without threatening community safety.

There are many models of security, guarding, policing and community safety that work. Some are illustrated in our report. Often, they apply to small areas for a limited time period. It is a question of applying widely and continually across city neighbourhoods what is known to work. The resources currently spent on crime-chasing and paper-pushing must be converted into crime prevention through street policing.

Many US cities have cut their violent crime by adopting a visible street presence and action against 'incivilities' (HUD, 1997). Our much smaller crime problems are certainly more manageable. Making urban dwellers feel 'comfortable and not alone' is an absolute key to regeneration.

Anti-social behaviour

As policing and security are enhanced, most forms of behavioural breakdown will shrink in proportion. Tougher enforcement in both cities is beginning to achieve this. But some people are so disturbed, so unhappy, so sick and out of control that they literally cannot help disrupting other people's lives. Some argue that there has been a fundamental erosion of our social fabric, particularly in inner cities, that many people are beyond normal help and, left alone, can only survive in a self-destructive, violent way (Davies, 1997). There may be some truth in this for a small minority. They must be protected from self-damage and communal havoc. Some institutional care is essential.

Formal community care arrangements can also work in less serious cases. Much care can come through informal supports and 'light handed' warden-assisted homes. The introduction of foyers and close supervision of tower blocks are examples we found of this new, caring approach in Newcastle. In Manchester, compacts with residents' groups are succeeding in holding the line on anti-social behaviour in very difficult areas.

The approach that always fails is housing vulnerable and unstable people within the most precarious neighbourhoods because there is space. It is an easy, short-term but self-defeating answer that local managers must have power to resist. Preventing the rehousing of unstable people was found to be a key to stabilisation in estates across Europe (Power, 1997). The extreme cases are few but far more resources must be dedicated to containing and helping them, not within areas already overloaded with social problems, but in a framework of specialised care as the government's recent increased support for mental health underlines (Department of Health, 1998).

The range of anti-social behaviour is frightening – harassment, arson, drug dealing, youth gangs, burglary, fights and other crime. Once it gets out of control, it is hard to stop as it appears to generate its own momentum. It is on this front that neighbourhoods are most likely to tip over the edge. But a combination of support, supervision and guarding measures gives a strong signal that people cannot abuse the neighbourhood. Essential measures we identified are:

- proactive policing
- custodial caretaking
- consistent enforcement
- screening of new lettings
- resident involvement in specific problems
- clear tenancy agreements
- co-operation between landlords and a multi-agency approach to problem-solving
- localised social supports
- special care and support for people with special needs
- family support.

Young men

Ideas about policing and behaviour breakdown underline the problems stemming from the loss of role for many men in low income urban communities (Power and Tunstall, 1997). Work patterns have changed in such a radical way that young men with low skills often no longer know where they fit in. They are heavy losers in the school system and the new job market (Social Exclusion Unit, 1998). It is a vast new social issue that receives too little focus and is building up into a longer-term problem.

Some of the trends are alarming – the loss of male jobs, the growth in lone parent female-headed families, the fear of youth gangs and the harassment of witnesses. In a report on the riots in the 1990s, we explored some of these issues (Power and Tunstall, 1997). A central lesson from that study was that communication and linkage can stop aggression and hostility from mounting to a point of inevitable breakdown.

The government's emphasis on education needs to do more than attack bad teachers and poorly performing schools; or help ambitious parents choose better schools; or reduce class sizes in the overcrowded (usually over-subscribed, better performing) schools. Tough, under-performing, inner city schools are often where special efforts are needed to help alienated, truanting and excluded boys, the children who start to fail on day one because of their environmental handicaps and never catch up. Investing more in those with greatest difficulties is expensive; the returns are uncertain, but the failures create far-reaching societal problems. Friendly, well structured secondary schools with a strong focus on core subjects, physical and social outlets, and parent involvement will help capture pupils' enthusiasm.

Many young people feel that society doesn't value them, that they are failures and a burden, or worse. This provokes immense hostility in youth which converts into aggressive attitudes towards adults and authority. Changing 'attitude' in youth requires confidence and the education of adults to deal with young people more positively. The voiceless/powerless/aggressive syndrome can be reversed (Power and Tunstall, 1997). This makes resident involvement, policing and local management essential to building bridges with young people. Linking things together so young men can get on the bridge is the most difficult of all, but it is doable.

Neighbourhood management or strategic vision?

When an area is pressured by many societal problems because of its position at the bottom of the urban hierarchy, intervention of a different kind is needed. A new kind of neighbourhood 'supremo', responsible for 'booting through' decisions, resources and actions, can be the pivot of integrated regeneration (Social Exclusion Unit, 1998). By definition, the neighbourhood 'supremo' needs to have real authority and a budget to act as a catalyst in changes (Ballymun Regeneration, 1998; Gregory, 1998).

The neighbourhood management idea has emerged from several experiences.

- It became a model for turning around some of the most difficult estates in Britain in the 1980s.

- The Social Exclusion Unit proposes it as a way of 'joining up' ground level services.

- European Rescue programmes, targeted at giant peripheral estates of up to 11,000 dwellings, successfully adopted this integrated, localised approach with a manager in charge (Power, 1999).

- In Britain, around £10 million of government *revenue* is spent each year on each estate of 1,000 dwellings (OECD, 1991). Making this 'work on the ground' to produce the caretaking, repairs, policing, training that estates need is elusive but crucial.

- Hands-on intensive management, pulling the patchwork of services, initiatives and ideas together, can have a dramatic impact.

- Successful experiments involve many services, but housing management is often in the lead because of the dominance of council landlords in the poorest areas.

- It only works across small areas where people identify a local interest.

- While area regeneration programmes are in train, a project manager can often play these roles. But neighbourhood management is about long-term, not short-term, inputs; about redirecting revenue already in the system, not

'special programmes'; about linking neighbourhoods into the wider system and developing fully a voice for local organisations and residents.

If key urban services were organised within a framework of neighbourhood management, leading to co-ordination and supervision, some of the most intractable problems would begin to shrink. The approach needs:

- a new framework
- experimentation
- independence – a project structure
- local authority commitment
- relatively small pump-priming
- strong political backing.

Figure 10 shows how neighbourhood management can provide local areas with intensive focused action linking them to the wider city. This requires external and government support – the top-down approach – combined with local services, community action and involvement – the bottom-up approach. We call this a patchwork model because the many small levers we found at work in neighbourhoods can together be made more powerful than the sum of the parts.

Figure 10 Patchwork model of neighbourhood change

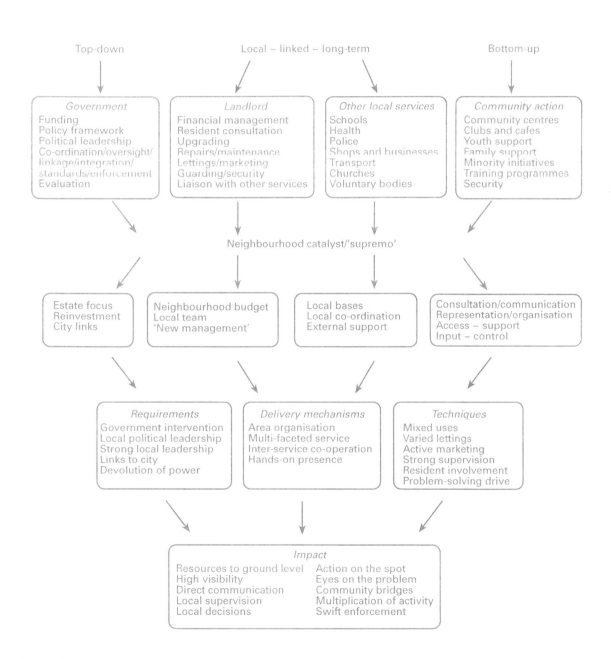

Source: Power, 1997.

14 Conclusion

This report documents an unexpected development in English cities. In spite of virtually continuous housing shortages from World War II to the mid-1970s, particularly in low income, urban communities, there is now clear evidence of housing abandonment within cities. This threatens and undermines the viability of the cities themselves and the survival of the neighbourhoods most affected. We studied the problem in detail in the North, but we gathered evidence of low demand for housing in neighbourhoods nationwide. The problem was most extensive in council estates. This development is occurring despite a large predicted growth in households and the argued need to build on greenfields.

The efforts to restore and regenerate inner neighbourhoods help to hold conditions and support remaining residents, but they have not yet reversed the outward flow of populations and jobs. Many historic factors had contributed:

- Britain's long industrial decline and economic restructuring leading to chronic unemployment and skill mismatch in cities
- Britain's interventionist slum clearance and mass council building programmes leading to the dominance of large, poor estates in inner cities
- long-term support for low-density, suburban owner occupation fuelling constant flight of higher earners.

Once a city exodus has gathered momentum, the most disadvantaged neighbourhoods at the bottom suffer disproportionate losses. This is often coupled with high demand in more popular areas.

The critical driving factors leading to actual abandonment are:

- the history and reputation of an area that deters ambitious newcomers
- the decayed environment
- easy access to better housing in better neighbourhoods
- the management problems facing local authorities
- the failure of mainstream services at the bottom
- the gradual breakdown of social stability leading to anti-social behaviour, crime and fear.

There is real potential for repopulating inner areas based on a shift in approach.

- We can build on the positive measures already in train.
- We need to reinforce our universal supports such as education, police and health, while targeting precarious areas with additional help.
- We need to market social housing to a wide band of the population to raise its value and increase demand.
- We need private owners to be involved in maintaining property and conditions.
- Regeneration projects can attract 'urban pioneers' back into centre cities and gradually spread into the increasingly empty inner neighbourhoods.
- It is central to encourage existing residents to stay and rebuild conditions as they provide an anchor for city rebirth.
- City densities need to be high to support services and create the street life that makes urban neighbourhoods attractive.

- We need to fit in many more small households to redensify our cities.

- Proactive policing can help to restore confidence, contain violence and reduce fear.

- Policing requires many channels of communications, local supports, clear ground rules and strong community links.

- In the end, urban neighbourhoods need an over-arching structure for managing conditions and orchestrating the constant changes.

Table 44 illustrates the tension between steep decline and renewal.

Many different approaches and initiatives work for neighbourhoods in trouble and many different buttresses are in place to sustain the web of interactions that keep communities alive. But national, regional, local authority and neighbourhood initiatives must link together in a continuous chain. Universal underpinning works only to the extent that the poorest people and most disadvantaged areas receive special help. 'Being relentless' and 'Doing it all' is the promise of the new government.

It is not inevitable that inner city areas will continue to lose people, control and viability. It is possible to make cities work. It is essential to the future of our environment, our communities and our crowded country that we invest more in saving what is clearly a huge but wasting asset. We must not leave inner city neighbourhoods in jeopardy. The ideas which this work stimulated are shown in Table 45.

Cities work through multiple enterprises, diverse households and communities. Stopping the spread of large urban poverty belts, as has happened in the US, is central to city growth, change and recovery (HUD, 1997; Jargowsky 1997). The neighbourhoods where we witnessed such acute decline may become the urban centres of tomorrow. They offer many assets: proximity; infrastructure; environmental potential; stable enclaves of residents holding on for a better future. It should not be beyond the wit and energy of our still highly urban, city focused society to lever in a new and better century for our cities.

Table 44 Current tensions in neighbourhood change

Threat – abandonment	Potential – renaissance
Economic and societal shifts	Intrinsic, undervalued assets
Skewed city populations	Community and civic leadership
Skewed city tenure structure	Fight-back, defending and developing city programmes
Strong polarisation	Reinvestment and rescue
Rapid decay of inner city neighbourhoods	Regeneration programmes
Growth in anti-social behaviour	Break-up of large council estates, open access
Crime, violence	Transfer to new social landlords
Fear and insecurity	City centre renewal and reclamation
Loss of cohesion and purpose	New urban pioneers
Incipient abandonment and demolition	People-based approaches

Table 45 Ideas for government action arising from the study

National	Regional	District	Neighbourhood
Increase density guidelines	Target inner and centre city regrowth	Link services and initiatives	Create neighbourhood 'supremo' to deliver neighbourhood management
Facilitate brownfield investment	Develop pro-city stance	Focus on major problem areas	Develop proposals for local housing companies to encourage investment
Pass true cost of greenfield development to developers	Propose brownfield plan	Develop local environmental plan including brownfield plan	
Develop urban transport	Intensify environmental agenda	Set environmental guidelines	Develop local police presence and liaison
Monitor demolitions and reduce incentives	Target worst first in parallel with general support	Develop special supports for families in difficulty	Collaborate with residents in all local initiatives
Proactively encourage tenure diversification	Target economic development, jobs	Advertise/market social housing	Create small seed-corn grant fund to support new ideas and continue supporting existing successful projects
Open up the allocation of social housing		Push tenure diversity	
Identify and ring fence revenue streams for local programmes		Create arm's length non-profit landlords on continental model to take on council housing	Target local budgets on local areas with devolved structures and decision-making
Target high demand regions for new housing		Develop neighbourhood management	Develop community plans, community compacts, local environment action plans
Equalise incentives for renovation with new build		Identify local revenue budgets	
Incentivise honesty in programme proposals and monitoring		Decentralise decisions and control	Screen lettings to all areas of concentrated disadvantage
		Help train resident activists	
Support incremental organic development		Support community development	Use local budgets to generate local jobs
Promote new ideas, structures		Promote proactive policing	Introduce super-caretaking
Push mixed uses, mixed incomes		Push training, investment	Involve schools in community
		Cut procedures and bureaucracy	Engage health visitors

Note: Tables 38 and 39 show the initiatives, policies and proposals already in train.

References

Atkinson, R. and Kintrea, K. (1998) *Reconnecting Excluded Communities: The Neighbourhood Impacts of Owner Occupation*. Edinburgh: Scottish Homes

Audit Commission (1989) *Urban Regeneration and Economic Development: The Local Government Dimension*. London: HMSO

Ballymun Regeneration (1998) *The Master Plan for Ballymun*. Dublin: Ballymun Regeneration

Best, R. (1998) Presentation to the Urban Task Force, Manchester, June

Blunkett, D. (1998) 'Launch of Education Action Zones', DfEE press release, 23 June

Bramley, G. (1998) 'Housing abandonment in the English inner city: housing surpluses and housing need', paper presented at conference, University of York, July

Briggs, A. (1983) *A Social History of England*. Harmondsworth: Penguin Books

Burbidge, M. (1992) Internal report on Scandinavian estate based services, DoE

Burbidge, M. *et al.* (1981) *An Investigation of Difficult to Let Housing*. London: DoE

Burchardt, T. and Hills, J. (1998) *Financial Services and Social Exclusion*. Insurance Trends: Quarterly Statistics and Research Review. London: Association of British Insurers

Burnett, J. (1978) *A Social History of Housing 1815–1970*. Newton Abbott: David and Charles

Burns, W. (1963) *New Towns for Old: The Technique of Urban Renewal*. London: Leonard Hill

Burrows, R. (1997) *Contemporary Patterns of Residential Mobility in Relation to Social Housing in England*. York: Centre for Housing Policy

Burrows, R. and Rhodes, D. (1998) *Unpopular Places? Area Disadvantage and the Geography of Misery in England*. Bristol: The Policy Press

Caisse des Depots (1998) Seminar at LSE, 23 November

Carley, M. and Kirk, K. (1998) *Sustainable by 2020? A Strategic Approach to Urban Regeneration for Britain's Cities*. Bristol: The Policy Press, with Joseph Rowntree Foundation

CASE (1998) Report to ESRC Conference on Social Exclusion, 2 December

Catholic Education Service (1997) 'A struggle for excellence: Catholic secondary schools in urban poverty areas', report prepared by the Committee for Community Relations of the Bishops' Conference of England and Wales

Central Statistical Office (1998) *Regional Trends*. London: HMSO

CHAC (Housing Management Sub-Committee of the Central Housing Advisory Committee of the Ministry of Housing and Local Government) (1939) *Management of Municipal Housing Estates: First Report*. London: HMSO

CHAC (1945) *Management of Municipal Housing Estates: Second Report*. London: HMSO

CHAC (1949) *Selection of Tenants and Transfers and Exchanges: Third Report*. London: HMSO

CHAC (1953a) *Living in Flats*. London: HMSO

CHAC (1953b) *Transfers, Exchange and Rents: Fourth Report*. London: HMSO

CHAC (1955a) *Residential Qualifications: Fifth Report.* London: HMSO

CHAC (1955b) *Unsatisfactory Tenants: Sixth Report.* London: HMSO

CHAC (1956) Moving *from the Slums: Seventh Report.* London: HMSO

CHAC (1959) *Councils and their Houses: Eighth Report.* London: HMSO

CHAC (1961) *Homes for Today and Tomorrow* (Parker Morris Report). London: HMSO

CHAC (1969) *Council Housing, Purposes, Procedures and Priorities: Ninth Report* (Cullingworth Report). London:HMSO

Chartered Institute of Housing (CIoH) (1998) *Low Demand for Housing Discussion Paper.* Coventry: CIoH

Cole, I. and Shayer, S. (1998) *Beyond Housing Investment: Regeneration, Sustainability and the Role of Housing Associations.* Sheffield: Centre for Regional Economic and Social Research, Sheffield Hallam University

Community Development Project (1976) *Whatever Happened to Council Housing?* London: Community Development Project Information and Intelligence Unit

Community Group Report[1] (1996) Tenants' survey results, November 1996

Council Report (1998) Report on new house building programme to Regeneration Board, 21 September

CPRE (1998) *Urban Exodus,* a report for CPRE prepared by T. Champion *et al.* London: CPRE

Crook, A.D.H., Darke, R.A. and Disson, J.S. (1996) *A New Lease of Life? Housing Association Investment on Local Authority Housing Estates.* Bristol: The Policy Press

Crossman, R. (1975) *The Diaries of a Cabinet Minister,* Vol. I. London: Hamish Hamilton and Jonathan Cape

Cullingworth, B. (1969) *Housing and Labour Mobility: A Preliminary Report.* Paris: OECD

Davies, N. (1997) *Dark Heart: The Shocking Truth about Hidden Britain.* London: Chatto and Windus Ltd

Daunton, M.J. (1987) *A Property Owning Democracy? Housing in Britain.* London: Faber

DETR (1997a) Monitoring information on demolitions

DETR (1997b) *Housing, Family and Working Lives.* Coventry: HMSO

DETR (1998a) *1998 Index of Local Deprivation.* London: DETR

DETR (1998b) *Planning for the Communities of the Future.* London: HMSO

DETR (1998c) *What Works – Learning the Lessons: Final Evaluation of City Challenge.* London: DETR

DETR (1998d) *Evaluation of the Single Regeneration Budget Challenge Fund – A Partnership for Regeneration: An Interim Evaluation.* London: DETR

DETR (1998e) *Consultation Paper A New Financial Framework for Local Authority Housing: Resource Accounting in the Housing Revenue Account.* London: DETR

DoE (1974) 'Difficult to let', unpublished report of postal survey

DoE (1977) *Inner Area Studies*. London: DoE

DoE (1981a) *Difficult to Let Investigation*. London: DoE

DoE (1981b) Report of visit to Newcastle for PEP

DoE (1996) *Urban Trends in England: Latest Evidence from the 1991 Census*. London: HMSO

DoE (1997) *Mapping Local Authority Estates Using the Index of Local Conditions*. London: DoE

Department of Health (1998) Press statement on additional funding for mental health, 10 December

Donnison, D. and Middleton, A. (1987) *Regenerating the Inner City: Glasgow's Experience*. London: Routledge and Kegan Paul

Downes, D. (ed.) (1989) *Crime and the City: Essays in Memory of John Barron Mays*. London: Macmillan

Dunleavy, P. (1981) *The Politics of Mass Housing in Britain 1945–75*. Oxford: Clarendon Press

(The) Economist (1998) *Economist* series on British cities, August

Ferris, J. (1972) *Participation in Urban Planning – the Barnsbury Case*. Occasional Papers on Social Administration (No. 46). London: G. Bell & Sons

Fielder, S. and Smith, R. (1996) *Vacant Dwellings in the Private Sector*. London: DoE

Fletcher, A. (1995) *Homes Still Wasted*. London: Empty Homes Agency

Foot, M. (1973) *Aneurin Bevan: A Biography, Vol. II 1945–1960*. London: Davis-Poynter

Forrest, R. and Murie, A. (1988) *Selling the Welfare State: The Privatisation of Public Housing*. London: Routledge

Gauldie, E. (1979) *Cruel Habitations: A History of Working-Class Housing, 1780–1918*. London: Allen & Unwin

Giddens, A. (1993) *The Consequences of Modernity*. Cambridge: Policy Press

Gladwell, M. (1996) 'The tipping point', *New Yorker*, 3 June

Glasgow District Council (Housing) (1986) *Inquiry into Housing in Glasgow*. Glasgow: City Press

Glennerster, H. and Hills, J. (1998) *The State of Welfare: The Economics of Social Spending*. Oxford: OUP

Greater London Council (GLC) (1979) Housing Committee minutes, GLC

Gregg, P. (forthcoming) Report of Treasury seminar on social exclusion

Gregory, S. (1998) *Transforming Local Services: Partnership in Action*. York: JRF

(The) Guardian (1999) 'The joy of tower blocks: electronic eyes turn seedy flats into des res', 6 January

Habitat (1996) *An Urbanising World*. Oxford: OUP for the United Nations Office on Human Settlements

Hackney Borough Council (1992) The Estate Action Form B submissions, August

Hall, P. (1989) *London 2001*. London: Unwin Hyman

Hall, P. (1990) *Cities of Tomorrow: An Intellectual History of Urban Planning and Design in the Twentieth Century*. Oxford: Blackwell

Hall, P. and Ward, C. (1998) *Sociable Cities: The Legacy of Ebenezer Howard*. New York: J. Wiley

Halsey, A.H. (ed.) (1988) *British Social Trends since 1900 – A Guide to the Changing Social Structure of Britain*. Coventry: HMSO

Hamilton, R. (ed.) (1976) *Street by Street*. London: North Islington Housing Rights Projects

Hills, J. (1998) *Thatcherism, New Labour and the Welfare State*. CASEpaper 13. London: CASE

Hobcraft, J. (1998) *Intergenerational and Life-course Transmission of Social Exclusion: Influences of Childhood Poverty, Family Disruption and Contact with the Police*. CASEpaper 15. London: CASE

Holland, Sir Milner (Chairman) (1965) *Report of the Committee on Housing in Greater London*. Cmnd 2605. London: HMSO

Holmans, A.E. (1987) *Housing Policy in Britain*. London: Croom Helm

Holmans, A.E. (1995) *Housing Demand and Need in England 1991–2011*. York: JRF

Home Office (1993–97) *Criminal Statistics England and Wales*. London: HMSO

Hough, M. and Tilley, N. (1998) *Getting the Grease to the Squeak: Research Lessons for Crime Prevention*. London: Home Office, Police Policy Directorate

House of Commons (1998) *A Brown and Pleasant Land: Household Growth and Brownfield Sites*. Report 117. London: Parliamentary Office of Science and Technology

Housing Corporation (1997) *Registered Social Landlords in 1996: General Report*. London: HC

Housing Services Advisory Group (HSAG) (1978) *Organising a Comprehensive Housing Service*. London: DoE

HUD (1997) *The State of Cities*. Washington: HUD

Hughes, J.W. and Sternlieb, G. (1987) *The dynamics of American Housing*. New Brunswicks, NJ: Rutgers

Hunt, R. and Kullberg, J. (1998) 'Dutch courage: advertising social housing in Britain', *Housing Agenda*, May

Huttman, E. and van Vliet, W. (1988) *Handbook of Housing and the Built Environment*. New York: Greenwood Press

Islington Borough Council (1976) *Estate Action Programmes on Unpopular Estates*. London: Islington Council

Jacobs, J. (1970) *The Death and Life of Great American Cities*. London: Cape

Jargowsky, P. (1997) *Poverty and Place: Ghettos, Barrios, and the American city*. New York: Russell Sage Foundation

Joseph Rowntree Foundation (1995) JRF Inquiry Group on Income and Wealth

Joseph Rowntree Foundation (1998a) *Foundations – Regenerating Neighbourhoods: Creating Integrated and Sustainable Improvements*. York: JRF

Joseph Rowntree Foundation (1998b) *Findings – Patterns of Neighbourhood Dissatisfaction*. York: JRF

Keenan, P. (1998) 'Housing abandonment and demand', paper presented at conference at University of York, July

Kiernan, K. (1997) *The Legacy of Parental Divorce: Social, Economic and Demographic Experiences in Adulthood*. CASEpaper 1. London: CASE

Konttinen, S. (1983) *Byker*. London: Jonathan Cape

Maclennan, D. (1991) *Paper on A Strategic Approach to Cities*. Edinburgh: OECD

Maclennnan, D. (1997) 'Britain's cities: a more positive future', Lunar Society lecture, November

Malpass, P. and Means, R. (eds) (1993) *Implementing Housing Policy*. Buckingham: Open University Press

Malpass, P. and Murie, A. (1994) *Housing Policy and Practice*. Basingstoke: Macmillan

Manchester and Newcastle (1998) Interviews with chief executives and directors of housing, September–October

Manchester City Council (1993) Manchester 1991 Census Ward Profiles

Manchester City Council (1996) 'Rehousing demand: report to Housing and Environmental Services Committee', 30 May

Manchester City Council (1997a) *Manchester Matters: Economic, Unemployment and Welfare Benefits Bulletin*, Summer

Manchester City Council (1997b) Neighbourhood renewal assessment[1]

Manchester City Council (1998a) Manchester's 1996 Local Census

Manchester City Council (1998b) New house building programme, report to Regeneration Board[1], September

Manchester City Council (1998c) Council report on neighbourhood options[1], October

Manchester City Council (1998d) Report on urban village in Ancoates Manchester

Manchester City Council (1998e) Observations to Joseph Rowntree advisory committee, 1 December

Manchester City Council (1998f) Evidence from Low Demand Team, December

Marris, R. (1996) *How to Save the Underclass*. Basingstoke: Macmillan

Modood, T., Berthoud, R., Lakey, J., Nazroo, J., Smith, P., Virdee, S. and Beishon, S. (1998) *Ethnic Minorities in Britain: Diversity and Disadvantage*. London: Policy Studies Institute

National House-Building Council Conference (1998) 'Sustainable housing – meeting the challenge', 11 September

NCHA (1998) *Thinking the Unthinkable: Delivering Sustainability in the North*. Chester le Street: NCHA

Newcastle and Manchester (1998) Statistics on Right to Buy sales supplied by City Councils

Newcastle City Council (1993) Newcastle City Profiles: results from the 1991 Census

Newcastle City Council (1994) Biennial residents' survey

Newcastle City Council (1997) Newcastle City Profiles: results from the 1996 Inter Censal Survey

Newcastle City Council (1998a) Internal proposals on combating social exclusion

Newcastle City Council (1998b) Tour with senior council officer, 12 November

Newcastle City Council (1998c) Unitary Development Plan

Newcastle City Council (1998d) 'A practical experience of building on the green belt', paper presented to the National Housing and Town Planning Conference, Carlisle, 14–16 July

Newcastle City Council (1998e) Report to Housing and Development Committees on industrial development opportunities

Newcastle City Council (1998f) Annual Review of Housing Development and Land Availability, report to Housing Committee, November

Northumbria Police (1998) Statistics supplied on local crime rates

OECD (1991) Seminar on liveable cities, Edinburgh, October

ONS (1990 and 1991) *Labour Force Survey/Great Britain*. London: ONS

ONS, DoE/Green, H. (1996) *Housing in England 1994/95*. A report of the 1994/95 Survey of English Housing carried out by the Social Survey Division of ONS on behalf of the DoE/ Hazel Green. London: HMSO

ONS (1997) *Social Trends*. London: HMSO

ONS (1998) Mid Census population projections reported in *The Guardian*, 8 December

OPCS (1984) 1981 *Census (Ward and Civil Parish Monitors)*. London: OPCS

OPCS (1992) *Census 1991: Definitions: Great Britain*. London: HMSO

OPCS (1994) *1991 Census (Ward and Civil Parish Monitors)*. London: OPCS

Pacione, M. (ed.) (1997) *Britain's Cities: Geographies of Division in Urban Britain*. London: Routledge

Pawson, H., Kearns, A., Keoghan, M., Malcolm, J. and Morgan, J. (1997) *Managing Voids and Difficult to Let Property*. London: The Housing Corporation

Peabody Trust (1996–98) Annual Reports

PEP (1981) *Improving Problem Council Estates: A Summary of Aims and Progress*. London: DoE

Plank, D. (ed.) (1998) *Joined up Thinking: A Directory of Good Practice for Local Authority Empty Property Strategies*. London: Empty Homes Agency

Poones, J., Schafer, R. and Hartman, C.W. (1980) *Housing Urban America*. New York: Aldine

Power, A. (1981) *Report on the Tulse Hill Estate for the Greater London Council*. London: PEP

Power, A. (1982) *Priority Estates Project 1982: Improving Problem Council Estates: A Summary of Aims and Progress*. London: DoE

Power, A. (1984) *Local Housing Management*. London: DoE

Power, A. (1987) *Property before People – The Management of Twentieth-century Council Housing.* London: Allen & Unwin

Power, A. with PEP Associates (1991a) *Housing Management: A Guide to Quality and Creativity.* London: Longman

Power, A. (1991b) *Running to Stand Still: Progress in Local Management on 20 Unpopular Housing Estates 1982–1988.* London: PEP Ltd

Power, A. (1993) *Hovels to High Rise.* London: Routledge

Power, A. (1995) *Perspectives on Europe.* London: Housing Corporation

Power, A. (1997) *Estates on the Edge.* London: Macmillan Press

Power, A. and Mumford, K. for the Housing Corporation (1999) Report of low demand seminar at the National Tenants' Resource Centre, convened by the Housing Corporation, September 1998

Power, A. and Tunstall, R. (1995) *Swimming against the Tide.* York: JRF

Power, A. and Tunstall, R. (1997) *Dangerous Disorder: Riots and Violent Disturbances in 13 Areas of Britain, 1991–92.* York: JRF

Prescott, J. (1998) Press release on launch of Urban Task Force. London: DETR

Prescott-Clarke, P., Clemens, S. and Park, A. for the DoE (1994) *Roots into Local Authority Housing: A Study of Local Authority Waiting Lists and New Tenancies.* London: HMSO

Prime Minister (1998) *The Government's Annual Report 1997/98.* London: The Stationery Office

Raynsford, N. (1999) Written communication to LSE Housing concerning urban sprawl, 15 February

Reich, R. (1993) *The Work of Nations: Preparing Ourselves for Twenty-first Century Capitalism.* New York: Vintage

Richardson, E. (1997) 'In the loop', report to the Trustees of the Gatsby Project. London: LSE Housing

Ridley, P. (1996) LSE housing seminar, November

Robson, B. (1995) *Inner Cities Research Project: Assessing the Impact of Urban Policy.* London: HMSO

Rogers, R. (1997) *Cities for a Small Planet.* London: Faber

Rudlin, D. (1998) *Tomorrow: A Peaceful Path for Urban Reform. The Feasibility of Accommodating 75% of New Homes in Urban Areas.* Manchester: UrbED

Sassen, S. (1998) *Globalisation and its Discontents.* New York: New Press

Saunders, P. (1990) *A Nation of Home Owners.* London: Unwin Hyman

Schussheim, M.J. (1974) *The Modest Commitment to Cities.* Lexington, MA: Lexington Books

Shelter (1998) Proposal to National Lottery on 'Homeless to Home' initiative

Social Exclusion Unit (1998) *Bringing Britain Together: A National Strategy for Neighbourhood Renewal.* London: The Stationery Office

Southwark Council (1994) *Peckham Partnership: A Bid for Single Regeneration Budget Funding,* prepared by the Partnership

Stegman, M.A. (1970) *Housing and Economics: The American Dilemma*. Cambridge, MA: MIT Press

Stegman, M.A. (1972) *Housing Investment in the Inner City: The Dynamics of Decline*. Cambridge, MA: MIT Press

Sternlieb, G. and Burchell, R. W. (1973) *Residential Abandonment: The Tenement Landlord Revisited*. New Brunswick, NJ: Rutgers

Thompson, F.H.J. (1990) *Cambridge Social History of Britain 1750–1950*, Vols 1, 2, 3. Cambridge: Cambridge University Press

Travers, A. (1998) 'Housing: high hopes' *The Guardian*, 17 June

Turok, I. and Edge, N. (forthcoming) *The Jobs Gap in British Cities*. York: JRF

Urban Splash (1998) *Live, Work, Play*. Liverpool: Urban Splash

Urban Task Force (1999a) Internal report of visit to Barcelona by the Urban Task Force

Urban Task Force (1999b) *Urban Renaissance – Sharing the Vision: Summary of Responses to the Urban Task Force Prospectus*. London: Urban Task Force

Vergara, C.J. (1997) *The New American Ghetto*. New Brunswick, NJ: Rutgers University Press

Wadhams, C. (1998) *Reinvestment Plus – Creating Thriving Neighbourhoods*. Birmingham: Chris Wadhams Associates

Webster, D. (1998) 'Employment change, migration and housing abandonment', paper presented to conference at Centre for Urban and Regional Studies, University of Birmingham, November

WHHA (1998) *Living in Town Report: Promoting the Housing Potential of London's High Streets*. London: West Hampstead Housing Association Ltd

Whitehead, C., Kleinman, M. and Chattrabhutti, A. (1995) *The Private Rental Housing Market: A Review of Current Trends and Future Prospects*. London: Council of Mortgage Lenders

Whitehead, C. (1998) Personal communication from Christine Whitehead, on the issue of private sector vacancies

Wilmott, P. and Young, M. (1957) *Family and Kinship in East London*. London: Routledge and Kegan Paul

Wilson, W.J. (1996) *Are Ghettos Emerging in Europe?* London: LSE Housing

Wilson, W.J. (1997) *When Work Disappears*. New York: Alfred A. Knopf

Wohl, A.S. (1977) *The Eternal Slum: Housing and Social Policy in Victorian London*. London: Edward Arnold

Wood, M. and Bryan, J. for the Northern Housing Research Partnership (1997) *Housing in the North: A Study of Empty Homes*. Chester-le-Street: Northern Consortium of Housing Authorities

Young, M. and Lemos, G. (1997) *Communities we Have Lost and Can Regain*. London: Lemos and Crane

Note

1 Names of specific local areas have been omitted to protect their identity.

Appendix 1

Interviews with local authorities and housing associations around the country

	Inner London LA	LA in South East	LA in South West	LA in West Midlands	HA in West Midlands	HA in Midlands region	HA in Eastern region	HA in Western region
Total stock		13,500	34,000	97,000	11,000	4,300	9,000	4,226
Voids		1.1% (142)	2.01%	2.23%				
Annual turnover			~ 10%	14% (1997/98)	20.7% (1997/98)	18% (1997/98)	15%	
Number on waiting list	6,428 new applicants (1997/98)	4,290 (of which 1,520 transfers)	16,100 on common housing register	36–40,000 (of which 26,000 = transfers)1997		Waiting lists inclusive; many areas have no waiting list at all.	2,000	
Changes in demand experienced	Disappearance of pressure from homeless households. More transient households applying.	Sheltered stock impossible to let. Homeless applications increased (but families reduced, single vulnerable increased).	Reducing demand for sheltered. Falling demand in a minority of general needs stock.	Increasing turnover in LA stock. Falling waiting list.	Dramatic increase in turnover (from 12% in 1996/97 to 21% in 1997/98) and abandonments (50% in 1997/98).	Dramatic increase in turnover (from 12% in 1996/97 to 18% in 1997/98).	Large scale voluntary transfer (LSVT) HA (1990). LA used receipt to build more houses – reduced demand for the flats.	New houses in one town in zero demand. Transient population on one estate (LSVT 1994).
Concentration of low demand?	Yes – unpopular estates.	Yes – 1-beds and bedsits – stigmatised estates (of which there are three main ones).	Yes, in sheltered stock; certain areas; certain property types (walk-up flats).	Yes – in areas with poor reputation and in unpopular stock types/ poor condition stock.	Yes – high turnover mainly in flats. Also stigmatised areas.	Yes – in stigmatised areas and estates (inc. new-build), and specific property types: 1-beds, bedsits, sheltered. poor terraces.	1,000 low demand properties due to: type, location, reputation. 25% turnover in this stock.	Yes – depends on location. Also, there is a surplus of single persons' accommodation.
Housing associations affected?	30% lets to homeless – only slightly higher than LA. HAs have street properties – not same issues as big estates.	Yes – in their sheltered stock and in their bedsits. Healthy demand for new-build.	Yes – with sheltered stock (the LA can't make nominations), and in certain areas.	Yes – see HA columns.	N/A	N/A	N/A	N/A

	Inner London LA	LA in South East	LA in South West	LA in West Midlands	HA in West Midlands	HA in Midlands region	HA in Eastern region	HA in Western region
Private housing affected?	No – very high prices. £150,000 – £200,000 for a house.	No – quite high demand even for poor quality private accommodation.	Slack during the recession. Some people who exercised the RTB having difficulty selling.	Yes – in certain pockets with bad reputation.			No – there has been a private sector boom.	
Any areas being 'abandoned'?	No.	No.	No – no areas with voids over 10%.	No.	No – can let virtually everything at present.	There are areas with very high incidence of voids relating to property type / stigmatised estate or streets. People just want to get out – 'should be demolished'.	No.	No.
Initiatives undertaken to combat low demand? Effect?	Advertising. Nothing is unsaleable / unlettable in London.	Conversion of sheltered bedsits to family-size accommodation – successful. Advertising of unpopular estate – successful. Marketing of sheltered bedsits – unsuccessful.	Demolition of multis, replacement by HAs. Redesign, security improvements – success. Letting to very low priority, under-occupying. Restricted number of offers to 3 – reduced average number of offers before acceptance.	Local allocation policies in selected areas – have reduced void turn-around period.	Home improvements. Stock swaps to rationalise stock. 'Deconversions'. Customer surveys. Plan to demolish some properties and rebuild. Local adverts – not good response.	Tower block refurbished, marketed, lettings quotas to achieve planned population profile of working, non-working, different age groups, etc. Successful. Developed this further – range of marketing packages for particular void types, regular ads, estate agent type boards, leaflet drops, locality and family and friends.	Taking strategic look at the stock – questioning whether demolition more sensible than refurbishment. About to knock down one block of flats. Considering outright sales of some stock.	

	Inner London LA	LA in South East	LA in South West	LA in West Midlands	HA in West Midlands	HA in Midlands region	HA in Eastern region	HA in Western region
Areas/stock types in high demand?	Yes.	Yes – especially street properties.	Yes – many areas very sought after.	Yes – including in some deprived areas.	Yes – but vast majority of stock in difficult inner city.	Yes – certain areas and 3-bed houses.	Yes – rationing model still applies to majority of stock.	Yes – pockets of high demand in certain locations.
Future concerns	The council owns too many properties.	The council has an over-supply of one-beds and bedsits.	Funding for further improvements.	Combination of high turnover, high number of unpopular design and urban exodus.	Research suggests property condition not reason for leaving – should redirect money to security measures.	Pace of change. Continued reduction in demand and increase in new voids each week. Huge debt portfolio to be financed.	Lack of adequate funding to demolish unpopular high-rise and bedsits.	Impact of anti-social behaviour, residents scared to get involved on one estate.
Future potential	Could open up waiting list to those not previously considered. In London, there is very high demand overall.	Marketing of flats to people not in housing need.	Looking at strategy for sheltered – different uses. Hoping to convert flats to family accommodation. Also to consolidate stock where LA and several RSLs in an area.	Change current restrictive access. Repackage to attract growing Asian population who currently have negative perception.	Still to try furnished accommodation. Beginning to share info with other RSLs.	Marketing, relaxing points threshold, developing scheme-specific lettings strategies, adapting working practices to changing situation – there is untapped housing demand.	Still to try local lettings and allowing under-occupation.	Marketing strategy not yet started.

Appendix 2
Additional interviews – contributors to low demand

	West Midlands LA	West Midlands HA	HA – Midlands region	South East LA	South West LA	Northern HA
Area factors						
Stigma/reputation	✔	✔	✔	✔	✔	✔
Crime rate/lack of feeling of security	✔	✔	✔	✔	✔	✔
Concentration of people living in poverty/lack of employment opportunities	✔	x	✔	✔	–	✔
Property factors						
Type of housing	✔'	✔'	✔'	√	✔	√
Poor physical property condition	✔	x	x	x	✔	√
Visible signs of vacancy, i.e. steel security	–	✔	✔	✔	✔	–
Service delivery factors						
Poor housing management by social landlords	–	x	x	–	x	–
Restrictive allocations policies	✔	–	✔	✔	–	✔
Reputation of schools	x	✔	√	✔	x	–
Lack of co-ordination between different service providers	–	–	x	x	x	–
Lack of shops	✔	x	√	✔	✔	–
City management factors						
Continued new-building by the LA/HAs	✔	–	✔	✔ (of sheltered)	–	✔
Inappropriately targeted regeneration programmes	–	–	–	✔	–	–
Building by the universities reducing student renter population	–	✔	–	x	x	–
National trends						
Urban exodus	✔	✔	✔	–	x	✔
Changing tenure aspirations/ availability of low cost owner occupation	✔	✔	✔	✔	✔	✔
Shift in the industrial base, with loss of jobs from the North	–	–	✔	–	–	✔

✔ = definite contributor

√ = contributes to some extent

x = does not contribute

– = not discussed

Appendix 3

Areas of the country with evidence of pockets of low demand, difficult to let properties and high turnover – affecting local authorities and/or housing associations (not exhaustive)

Wakefield	Liverpool
Sheffield	Sandwell
Birkenhead	Coventry
Blackburn	Birmingham
Bradford	Wolverhampton
Stockton	Nottingham
Middlesbrough	Bedford
Sunderland	Bristol
Gateshead	Lambeth
Cleveland and Redcar	Southwark
Hull	Hackney
Salford	Islington*
Wigan	Hammersmith and Fulham*
Knowsley	Brent
Burnley	Haringey
Kirklees	Greenwich
Carlisle	Lewisham
Bolton	Thurrock
Leeds	Brighton

* Generally high demand areas, but with specific unpopular estates.

Appendix 4
Other current research

Bramley, G., 'Housing surpluses and housing need', paper presented to conference at University of York, July 1998

CIoH, 'Low demand for housing – discussion paper', paper presented to conference at University of York, July 1998

DETR/Bramley, G., 'Low demand for housing and unpopular neighbourhoods', research commenced October 1998

Keenan, P., 'Housing abandonment and demand', paper presented to conference at University of York, July 1998

Lowe, S., 'Housing abandonment in the English Inner City', paper presented to conference at University of York, July 1998

Murie, A., Nevin, B. and Leather, P., 'Changing demand and unpopular housing', Working Paper No. 4, Housing Corporation, 1998

Pawson, H., 'Residential instability and tenancy turnover', paper presented to conference at University of York, July 1998

Research and Change! Consultancy, 'Frequent movers' study (Joseph Rowntree Foundation, forthcoming)

Stringer, F. (Manchester Housing), 'Area based housing management and corporate responses to low housing demand', paper presented to conference at University of York, July 1998

Webster, D., 'Employment change, migration and housing abandonment', paper presented to conference at University of Birmingham, November 1998

Appendix 5
Schedule of fieldwork interviews

	No. of people
Two cities and four neighbourhoods	
Central senior staff	6
Staff in the following services:	
Housing (LA)	22
Housing (HA)	21
Education	9
Police	12
Social Services	3
Community/leisure	3
Regeneration/private sector renewal	11
Councillors	4
Voluntary sector	5
Private sector (shops and estate agents)	3
Academics	5
Residents	24
Total	**128**
Outside the two cities	
LA staff	15
HA staff	13
Voluntary sector	5
Total	**33**

Manchester City Council

Corporate Aims

Manchester City Council aims to continue to create a City of national and international significance where people choose to live and in which companies want to invest; a City where all citizens benefit from regeneration and have equal access to the wealth, employment and other opportunities which this brings.

The Council further aims to improve the health, security and quality of life of its citizens by promoting and supporting sustainable communities which are safe, friendly and clean.

The City Council will work to ensure that residents receive high quality services which meet their needs and will also form active relationships with others in the private, voluntary and other parts of the public sectors to promote whatever initiatives are in the interests of the City.

The City Council takes its role as the only democratically elected and accountable body in the City very seriously. It undertakes to consult widely in order that the views and interests of all citizens are fully represented in the planning and future development of the City.

The Council is committed to putting equality of opportunity at the heart of everything it does.

Manchester
making it happen

Corporate Objectives

1. The Economy
To increase economic activity in the City by rebuilding and enhancing the City Centre, increasing investment, creating jobs, developing a skilled workforce and promoting technological growth.

Key Performance Indicators include: progress on rebuilding City Centre, levels of inward investment, numbers of jobs created, unemployment levels and levels of benefit dependency.

2. Population
To increase the numbers of people living in the City, including the City Centre, and to stabilise the population in unpopular neighbourhoods by reducing housing turnover.

Key Performance Indicators include: population numbers, housing turnover, residential levels in the City Centre.

3. Crime
To lead the development of community safety strategies which reduce crime and help people to feel safer.

Key Performance Indicators include: comparative surveys to establish how safe people feel.

4. Health
To develop, in conjunction with relevant health agencies, strategies to prevent ill-health and improve the health of the population.

Key Performance Indicators include: changes/improvements in areas such as child dental health, birth weight, and reduction in the years of life lost as a result of coronary heart disease.

5. Quality
To promote high quality in the delivery of Council services.

Key Performance Indicators include: Performance against the Council's own Standards of Service and Statutory Performance Indicators, decreases in recorded complaints and increases in compliments, staff attitudes to the importance of high quality services.

6. Educational Standards
To improve educational attainment at all levels of the school system and to increase staying-on rates into Further and Higher Education.

Key Performance Indicators include: Performance in Standard Assessment Tests and national examinations, number of school leavers entering F.E. and H.E. and drop out rates.

7. Image and Perception
To improve the image of Manchester, to both residents and non-residents, as a City which is attractive as a place in which to live and invest and to visit.

Key Performance Indicators include: results of surveys of people's perception and feelings about the City.

Manchester
making it happen

Appendix 7
Newcastle's corporate strategic plan: key extracts

The City Council's vision for Newcastle

- An accessible city with equal opportunity for all its people to realise their potential through education, work, and other activities without discrimination or fear.

- A city which provides a safe, clean, healthy and sustainable environment.

- A city where residents take an active part in the democratic process and participate in decisions about their public services, their local community and their quality of life.

- A city which values its rich culture, heritage and strong sense of identity.

- A city which is regional capital of the North East and which continues to build links with Europe.

Core values and beliefs

The City Council is committed to:

- The value of public service provided by democratically accountable local government.

- The best use of its resources for the benefit of all residents whilst recognising the particular needs of the poorest, most vulnerable and disadvantaged.

- The vital importance of social, economic, and cultural regeneration to improve the quality of life and opportunity for the people of Newcastle.

- The value of working in partnership with community, business, and voluntary organisations, with government departments and with other agencies to achieve the best for our community.

- Equality of opportunity for people from all of Newcastle's diverse communities, ensuring that we treat all people with sensitivity, fairness and respect.

- Providing services that are easily accessible, responsive, relevant and good value for money, and opportunities for people to participate in the development of better services.

- Creating an accessible and suitable environment offering mobility to all.

- Providing clear information about the standards that Council services should meet.

- Recognising people's right to complain and have things put right.

The Council's priorities

Corporate policy priorities

Priority 1: Educational achievement
Raising levels of attainment and improving educational standards for all learners in the City.

Priority 2: Tackling youth and long-term unemployment
Implementing Welfare to Work and reducing unemployment amongst young people and long-term unemployment overall.

Priority 3: Community regeneration

Social, economic and cultural regeneration of local areas which are suffering or likely to suffer decline.

Priority 4: Improving the local environment

Working to create a clean, healthy and attractive environment which will improve the quality of life in Newcastle.

Priority 5: The City as regional and cultural capital of the North East

Retaining and developing Newcastle's role as regional capital in terms of retailing, entertainment, cultural facilities and employment opportunities.

Cross-functional guiding principles

1 *Best value*

The commitment to quality and continuous improvement in everything we do.

2 *Equal opportunities and accessibility*

The commitment to provide services fairly to all people in the community, improve access to those services, and ensure that we act as an equal opportunities employer.

3 *Local Agenda 21*

The commitment to minimise the use of non-renewable resources and promote recycling of waste whilst working towards building sustainable communities.

4 *Community participation and involvement*

The commitment to promote and facilitate the active participation of Newcastle residents in decision making and the development of community planning.

Appendix 8
Articles about low demand and abandonment

Date	Source	Article
Oct. 95	Daily Telegraph	Escaping from cities
06/07/96	The Economist	The cities come back to life
22/11/96	Manchester Evening News	Unpopular council homes suffering from decay are to be demolished and replaced
04/12/96	The Guardian	Providing an extra 4.4 million households by 2016 is a pipe dream (Peter Hall)
11/12/96	The Independent	The buck stops here
1996	Birmingham City Council	Movement of people out of the city
Jan./Feb. 97	Roof	More than 500 HA schemes are difficult to let
22/01/97	Housing Today	Housing demand level is an overestimate
22/01/97	Housing Today	Coulter dismisses green belt scaremongers
22/01/97	Housing Today	Selecting the right solutions on need
22/01/97	Housing Today	Just because it's there – the lack of financial strategy in housing
22/01/97	Housing Today	A chance to get a piece of the action – SRB funding
23/01/97	Inside Housing	Association buys in extra patrol from Manchester police
23/01/97	Inside Housing	Empties lobby hails VAT harmony
Mar. 97	Housing	Empty houses (John Turney)
Jun. 97	The Housing Magazine	Put the people first
Jun. 97	The Housing Magazine	Who wants social housing?
02/06/97	Townscape and urban design	Quality of life in cities
13/06/97	Inside Housing	Conquering the Viking – stopping abandonment on an estate in Sheffield
Jul. 97	Housing	Key ingredient is ensuring access to work on a sustainable basis
Jul. 97	Housing	Closing the gap between rich and poor
11/07/97	Inside Housing	Low demand will see 400 homes demolished (Newcastle)
25/07/97	Inside Housing	Lack of investment sparks Cardiff rampage
01/08/97	Inside Housing	Teens face supervision
01/08/97	Inside Housing	Welcoming the new focus on communities
08/08/97	Inside Housing	Call to set targets on empties
15/08/97	The Pink Paper	Salford – cluster of tower blocks let to gay and lesbian people
15/08/97	Inside Housing	Tower blocks in Newcastle very popular with vulnerable people
15/08/97	Inside Housing	Whole estates could spiral downwards because of drug dealing presence
21/08/97	Housing Today	Councils keen to hang on to nomination function
22/08/97	Inside Housing	CPRE – local authorities make over-provision on greenfield sites
22/08/97	Inside Housing	Many benefits of short-term social housing have been overlooked
22/08/97	Inside Housing	A rent free month on one of Coventry MDC's most run down estates
Sep. 97	Housing	London housing need
Sep. 97	Roof	Would Britain gain from French style targeting of resources? (Jim Dickson)
Sep. 97	Housing	Mixed tenure estates only have an effect when % of shared ownership is high
12/09/97	Inside Housing	Calls for the building of new towns similar in scale to that of the post war period
12/09/97	Inside Housing	Promoting tenant training regime, exploring neighbour problems
12/09/97	Inside Housing	The last resort – some people prefer to remain in B&B than live in hard to let
12/09/97	Inside Housing	Ultimatum issued on empty properties – Norwich DC and Norfolk CC
17/09/97	The Times	Half of all LA and HA rented properties are now workless
18/09/97	Hull Mail	Bid to move tenants into no-go areas (Angus Young)
18/09/97	Housing Today	Local housing strategies – HAs and LAs not working well together

Date	Source	Article
18/09/97	Housing Today	Bentilee estate, plans to break up estate into 5 villages and get people back to work
18/09/97	Housing Today	Survey of 25 LAs and 9 HAs on social exclusion
18/09/97	Housing Today	Domestic violence and family disputes are contributing to increase in older homeless
18/09/97	Housing Today	Choosing the right location for new homes can tackle deprivation
19/09/98	Inside Housing	Liverpool HAT wants to use council waiting list to fill half empty blocks
19/09/97	Inside Housing	Older people and homelessness – unable to sustain mortgage repayments
19/09/97	Inside Housing	Hull – success with professional witnesses – eviction of drug dealer
19/09/97	Inside Housing	Knocking down estates could be a better option
19/09/97	Inside Housing	EHA-accredited letting scheme brings thousands of empty homes back into use
26/09/97	Inside Housing	Empty homes hotline to be launched in November
26/09/97	Inside Housing	Birmingham MDC 94 million regeneration scheme
Oct-97	Housing	Planning system is a land value lottery (Charmaine Young)
01/10/97	The Guardian	Leeds – vandalised home on the market for 1,000 pounds
02/10/97	Housing Today	Are we able to protect and preserve all communities? (Ged Lucas)
02/10/97	Housing Today	Setting the targets for change-need mix of area targeting and national policies
02/10/97	Housing Today	Hilary Armstrong wants to see a range of policy options before turning to the bulldozer
03/10/97	Inside Housing	Doubt cast on impact of renewal schemes – Association of London Government
03/10/97	Inside Housing	Government pledges to tackle social exclusion through housing
03/10/97	Inside Housing	Dept. of Transport owns hundreds of empty properties awaiting road building decisions
03/10/97	Inside Housing	CIoH priority survey – regeneration of deprived estates, repairs, bringing empties into use
09/10/97	Inside Housing	Can contracts of mutual support recreate communities? (Micheal Young and Gerard Lemos)
10/10/97	Inside Housing	Merseyside – how residents, council officers and police cleared drug dealers
16/10/97	Housing Today	Task force to improve city centre living launched by Leeds City Council
16/10/97	Housing Today	Credit unions could play a vital role in tackling social exclusion
16/10/97	Housing Today	Openness by both LA and HA key to a successful partnership
16/10/97	Housing Today	Councils to get HA information
16/10/97	Housing Today	Warwick – find it fill it scheme, reward to people who report empties which are filled
16/10/97	Housing Today	Sheltered housing – can't nominate or won't nominate?
17/10/97	Inside Housing	Fraud families to be targeted – families who switch homes to cheat or benefits
17/10/97	Inside Housing	Bradford City Challenge a 10 million flop – could not attract working people to live in estate
17/10/97	Inside Housing	Knock down sink estates and sell land – Nationwide Building Society
17/10/97	Inside Housing	Could bulldozers become the professionals' best friend? (Julian Dobson)
17/10/97	Inside Housing	ERCF – demand important factor – linked to geography (Jeff Zitron)
23/10/97	Housing Today	Growing demand for fully furnished lettings
24/10/97	Inside Housing	Estates have had their day (J. McCarron, Glasgow Council's housing chair)
30/10/97	Housing Today	Lettings Plus – tackling the problem of empty properties and helps non-priority homeless
31/10/97	Inside Housing	Edinburgh – 60% of offers fail to result in new tenancies
Nov. 97	Housing	Too many empty homes in Scotland
Nov. 97	Housing	In creating communities, planners need to look backwards (David Lunts)
06/11/97	Housing Today	Northern providers ask for greater freedom to spend funds on community regeneration
06/11/97	Housing Today	Tax breaks urged for derelict land – CPRE
06/11/97	Housing Today	Inability to furnish accommodation main reason for not remaining in LA homes
07/11/97	Inside Housing	Sunderland MDC plans to ban bad tenants from its waiting list

Date	Source	Article
07/11/97	Inside Housing	Fewer homeless families placed in temp. B&B by Nottingham council
07/11/97	Inside Housing	Massive potential for converting empty office space into low cost housing
13/11/97	Housing Today	Housing need increasing in the North (Martin Wood)
13/11/97	Housing Today	Ridding social housing of stigma and regenerating inner cities' key challenges
13/11/97	Housing Today	Working on empties is getting results (Bob Lawrence)
13/11/97	Housing Today	First eviction of an introductory tenant has happened
14/11/97	Inside Housing	Community consultation is possible (Steve Gayle)
14/11/97	Inside Housing	HAs must rein back their development aspirations (David Cowans, North British HA)
14/11/97	Inside Housing	HAs must plan ahead to stave off the threat of a lettings crisis (Simon Dow)
14/11/97	Inside Housing	Housing investment a waste of money unless we put youth first (Anthony Mayer)
14/11/97	Inside Housing	Tenants that feel good about living in an area will make an estate last (Julian Dobson)
14/11/97	Inside Housing	Figures suggesting 4.4 million homes questioned by Labour MP David Drew
21/11/97	Inside Housing	Manchester puts its faith in youth for future lettings
21/11/97	Inside Housing	Regeneration policy a failure (DETR)
27/11/97	Housing Today	Tenants back plan to transfer a Manchester City Council estate to an HA
27/11/97	Housing Today	Exclusion study shows widening gap (Demos)
27/11/97	Housing Today	Government still considering what the target for new housing will be
27/11/97	Housing Today	Regeneration scheme has turned Stockwell Park estate into a lovely place
27/11/97	Inside Housing	Some properties need to be demolished (Stephen Porter)
Dec-97	National Housing Awards	Best Funding Solution – Empty homes strategy – London Borough of Brent
04/12/97	Housing Today	Shelter warns of unimaginable homeless crisis in Scotland
05/12/97	Inside Housing	Reverse cuts or face homeless explosion – Shelter Scotland
11/12/97	Housing Today	Private sector is leading the fight against empties – Empty Homes Agency
11/12/97	Housing Today	Growth in home ownership is likely to slow significantly in Britain over next 20 years
12/12/97	Inside Housing	Midlands lacks the space for 5,000 extra homes – West Midlands regional forum
12/12/97	Inside Housing	Street sleepers need more than a roof – Homeless Network
12/12/97	Inside Housing	8,900 homes in England created by conversions
12/12/97	Inside Housing	Governments will have to balance building new homes and curbing Housing benefit
12/12/97	Inside Housing	MPs to scrutinise the Government's assessment of housing need
12/12/97	Inside Housing	HA development grants are at the right level – National Housing Federation study
19/12/97	Inside Housing	Question the need to provide 4.4 million homes
19/12/97	Inside Housing	Laws to deal with empty properties (Scotland)
09/01/98	Inside Housing	Need figure rises to 5.5 million
09/01/98	Inside Housing	Ask what we are building, where and for whom?
15/01/98	Hackney Gazette	Empty property team getting empty private homes back into use – Hackney Council
20/01/98	The Independent	Prescott proposes Green Belt Tax
24/01/98	The Independent	Government urged to build new homes on brownfield sites
26/01/98	The Times	Fewer houses may be built on farmland
Feb. 98	Housing	Number of priority homeless falls
12/02/98	Housing Today	New estimates fuel confusion
12/02/98	Housing Today	Why BMW drivers hold the key
12/02/98	Housing Today	Empty stock
13/02/98	Inside Housing	Coalition in battle to end VAT on empties

Date	Source	Article
19/02/98	Housing Today	Councils to offer homes to private sector tenants
19/02/98	Housing Today	Panicking planners
20/02/98	Inside Housing	Empty homes soar
26/02/98	Housing Today	Report shows mass urban exodus
27/02/98	Inside Housing	Brownfield target fails to address social need
27/02/98	Inside Housing	Demolition may prove cheapest
27/02/98	Inside Housing	Negative value sale hopes rise
27/02/98	Inside Housing	The numbers game – Gov. statistics on housing need based on outdated ideology
04/03/98	DETR	Local authorities urged to renovate and cut the number of empty homes
14/03/98	The Independent	The lesson from the underclass
19/03/98	Housing Today	Let us break out of this climate of fear – changing needs in housing
20/03/98	Inside Housing	Market forces – tenants turning their backs on social housing
20/03/98	Inside Housing	Hard sums – will new homes be affordable?
20/03/98	Inside Housing	Office politics – empty homes and offices are vital in meeting future housing demand
26/03/98	Housing Today	Prescott's new build plan lacks ambition
26/03/98	Housing Today	Carrot for well-behaved tenants
27/03/98	Inside Housing	Pressure to perform – empty homes are becoming a serious problem for social landlords
02/04/98	Housing Today	Lone parents go private
03/04/98	Inside Housing	Calling time on crime – councils given new duties to fight anti-social behaviour
03/04/98	Inside Housing	Flats stay empty as tenants pick and choose
09/04/98	Inside Housing	A chance that we must take – housing professionals influencing the agenda
17/04/98	Inside Housing	Government plans for more affordable homes
23/04/98	Housing Today	Housing's wasted years – cash should not be invested in no hope areas
23/04/98	Housing Today	Pleas for the extension of child curfew schemes
24/04/98	Inside Housing	No-hope homes to go
30/04/98	Housing Today	Empty property rate to encourage landlords
11/05/98	DETR press notice	Bringing empty buildings back into use is at the heart of the Government's approach
14/05/98	Housing Today	Crime, unemployment, lack of facilities are top of people's agenda
15/05/98	Inside Housing	Don't repeat the mistakes of the past (letter) (Dave Brown)
21/05/98	Housing Today	Rural Housing Trust building balanced communities (letter) (Patricia Phipps)
21/05/98	Housing Today	Wrong to stop investing in new homes in the North East (letter) (Andrea Titterington)
21/05/98	Housing Today	Revolutionising housing strategy
22/05/98	Inside Housing	People do not want to live in homes that are visually identifiable as social housing
22/05/98	Inside Housing	North needs new homes (letter) (Andrea Titterington)
29/05/98	Inside Housing	Don't cast the North East adrift (letter) (David Butler)
Jun. 98	Housing	How high self-esteem can be returned to social housing
Jun. 98	Housing	Public relations and housing
Jun. 98	Housing	More people being marginalised by being excluded from social housing
Jun. 98	The Guardian	Parents place tearaways in care to avoid eviction
04/06/98	Housing Today	Tackling the needs of young people on housing estates
04/06/98	Housing Today	Housing staff join police drug team
05/06/98	Inside Housing	Experts hide abandonment of houses
11/06/98	Housing Today	Witnesses still not safe

Date	Source	Article
11/06/98	Housing Today	Tenant bans create social exclusion
12/06/98	Inside Housing	Sunderland MDC rejects accusations that its get-tough policy has put young people in care
12/06/98	Inside Housing	Shelter claims councils abuse exclusion powers
12/06/98	Inside Housing	Manchester rethinks limit on repairs for nuisance tenants
26/06/98	Inside Housing	Associations face end of private cash
26/06/98	Inside Housing	Unwanted homes don't justify cuts
26/06/98	Inside Housing	Task force shocked by dreadful pit homes
26/06/98	Inside Housing	Supercaretakers to the rescue
02/07/98	Housing Today	Downturn in demand
02/07/98	Housing Today	Foyers have been built in the wrong places
17/07/98	Inside Housing	Why are local authority homes so undesirable?
17/07/98	Inside Housing	MoD's empty homes
23/07/98	Housing Today	No easy answers for low demand northern estates
23/07/97	Housing Today	As safe as houses – security in Oldham
24/07/98	Inside Housing	New chiefs to fight disorder
24/07/98	Inside Housing	Councils hit by abandonment
30/07/98	Housing Today	Take a more balanced look at issues facing the North
30/07/98	Housing Today	Reshape high streets before it's too late
30/07/98	Housing Today	Neighbourhoods for richer and for poorer
31/07/98	Inside Housing	Challenge on empties
Jul./Aug. 98	Housing	Sin bin creates model citizens – Dundee families project
03/08/98	The Guardian	Billions wasted on unwanted homes
14/08/98	Inside Housing	Sanctuary tries commercial approach to tackle voids
27/08/98	Housing Today	Comment on MoD homes
10/09/98	Inside Housing	Lessons from the letting agents – benefits of private landlords
11/09/98	Inside Housing	Gateshead deserves applause for vetoing new homes – editorial
11/09/98	Inside Housing	Housing staff ignored by social services
11/09/98	Inside Housing	Gateshead halts building
18/09/98	Inside Housing	Converting commercial buildings to residential use is slowing down in London
19/09/98	Inside Housing	Councils that cannot find tenants
01/10/98	The Economist	Affordable homes must be given higher priority
01/10/98	Housing Today	Social housing becoming a greater risk to lenders
02/10/98	Inside Housing	New scheme could be a key to unlock the potential of empty homes
02/10/98	Inside Housing	Residents treating council housing as a short term option
23/10/98	Inside Housing	Glasgow City Council looking to a trust to solve its problems
02/12/98	The Guardian	Prescott in clash over new home tax

Appendix 9

Local authority stock size, number of difficult to let units, empties, demolitions for Manchester and Newcastle

	Manchester		Newcastle	
	1990	1997	1990	1997
Council stock	93,475	78,929	43,678	38,196
Difficult to let property	14,804 (1991)	10,750 (1996)	2,810 (1991)	5,624 (1996)
Empty property	5,574	2,582	2,473	1,674
% of LA stock empty	6.0	3.3	5.7	4.4
% empty private property	4.7	6.6	6.2	5.8
Amount of the LA stock demolished between 1991 and 1998	1,791		1,644	
% of 1991 stock demolished[1]	2		4	
Volume of empty council stock in 1998	4,744 (6%) (November)		1,774 (4.8%) (October)	

Source: Annual HIP returns from DETR, Newcastle and Manchester Housing Departments.

1 This figure does not include all regeneration-driven demolitions.

The figures for empty property raise some important questions. The fall between 1990 and 1997 does not correspond with the evidence at neighbourhood level. It may be partly explained by large regeneration schemes which remove unpopular properties from normal management while being 'regenerated' or awaiting action. It may also be that the government's strict monitoring of performance indicators encourages local authorities to class empty properties as 'awaiting major repair/renewal' rather than as 'void'. Better monitoring of voids and more proactive marketing has also helped. Both cities report chronic low demand for much of their stock.